sma

GOD'S STORY
part 1

The Old Testament

THE
GOSPEL
PRO✝ECT
FOR ADULTS

LifeWay | Adults

Ed Stetzer General Editor Trevin Wax Managing Editor

No part of this work may be reproduced or transmitted in any form or by any means, electronic or mechanical, including photocopying and recording, or by any information storage or retrieval system, except as my be expressly permitted in writing by the publisher. Requests for permission should be addressed in writing to LifeWay Press®, One LifeWay Plaza, Nashville, TN 37234-0175.

ISBN: 978-1-4300-2521-4
Item: 005582520

Dewey Decimal Classification Number: 220.07
Subject Heading: BIBLE—STUDY \ THEOLOGY—STUDY \ GOSPEL—STUDY

We believe that the Bible has God for its author; salvation for its end; and truth, without any mixture of error, for its matter and that all Scripture is totally true and trustworthy. To review LifeWay's doctrinal guideline, please visit *www.lifeway.com/doctrinalguideline*.

Unless otherwise noted, all Scripture quotations are taken from the Holman Christian Standard Bible®, copyright 1999, 2000, 2002, 2003, 2009 by Holman Bible Publishers. Used by permission.

To order additional copies of this resource, write to LifeWay Church Resources; One LifeWay Plaza; Nashville, TN 37234-0113; phone toll free (800) 458-2772; fax (615) 251-5933; e-mail *orderentry@lifeway.com*; order online at *www.lifeway.com*; or visit the LifeWay Christian Store serving you.

Printed in the United States of America.

Adult Ministry Publishing
LifeWay Church Resources
One LifeWay Plaza
Nashville, Tennessee 37234-0175

Table of Contents

Writers

Part 1: Foundations

Halim Suh and his wife, Angela, have three kids and live in Austin, Texas, where he is pastor of equipping at The Austin Stone Community Church. He is the author (with Matt Carter) of two Threads studies: *Creation Unraveled* and *Creation Restored*. Halim has a Master of Divinity from Southwestern Baptist Theological Seminary.

Part 2: God Develops His Covenant People

Jonathan Leeman lives with his wife and three daughters in Cheverly, Maryland, where he is a member at Capitol Hill Baptist Church in Washington, DC. He is the author of *Reverberation: How God's Word Brings Light, Freedom, and Action to His People* and the editorial director for 9Marks Ministries. Jonathan has a Master of Divinity from The Southern Baptist Theological Seminary.

Part 3: God's Covenant People Divided, Scattered, and Brought Back

Christian George is assistant professor of biblical and theological studies at Oklahoma Baptist University. He is the author of *Sex, Sushi, & Salvation*, *Godology*, and *Sacred Travels*. He earned his PhD from the University of St. Andrews in Scotland.

The Gospel Project

Introduction

Some people see the Bible as a collection of stories with morals for life application. But it is so much more. Sure, the Bible has some stories in it, but it is also full of poetry, history, codes of law and civilization, songs, prophecy, letters—even a love letter. When you tie it all together, something remarkable happens. A story is revealed. One story. The story of redemption through Jesus. **This is** *The Gospel Project.*

When we begin to see the Bible as the story of redemption through Jesus Christ, God's plan to rescue the world from sin and death, our perspective changes. We no longer look primarily for what the Bible says about us but instead see what it tells us about God and what He has done. After all, it is the gospel that saves us, and when we encounter Jesus in the pages of Scripture, the gospel works on us, transforming us into His image. **We become God's gospel project.**

Core Values

Deep, but Not Dry

We believe it's best to expect a lot out of those who attend a small group. We don't need to go only as deep as the least knowledgeable person in the group. We may have to "cut up the meat" for new believers and make sure the truth is accessible, but the important thing is that everyone has been fed and is sufficiently nourished.

Christ-Centered

God is the primary Actor in the grand narrative of Scripture, and the gospel of Jesus Christ is the climax of this story. We approach the Old Testament as Jesus did: all the Scriptures testify to Him. We approach New Testament ethics and commands as implications that flow from the gospel—Christ crucified and raised.

Story-Focused

Being Christ-centered naturally brings our focus to the overarching story that the Bible tells in four parts: Creation / Fall / Redemption / Restoration. This helps us connect the dots in the great story that tells the truth about our world and provides a hope-filled outlook on our world because of the future God has promised.

Mission-Driven

Telling the story of the Bible is impossible without leading to mission, as the gospel reveals the heart of our missionary God and His desire to save people of every tribe, tongue, and nation. Keeping a focus on how the gospel leads us to mission is a crucial aspect of how we apply the Bible to our lives.

Part 1

FOUNDATIONS

In the beginning, God created the heavens and the earth. Everything was good; man enjoyed perfect harmony with the creation, with each other, and with God. Yet in the midst of that harmony, man sinned against God and fractured God's good creation, resulting in curses, exile, and death. But God made a covenant that would result in blessing, restoration, and resurrection.

Chapter 1

Creation

The Story Begins

"To fill the whole world with his image-bearers who know him, trust him, depend on him, and enjoy him was and is the mission of God in creation."[1]
  –Keith Whitfield

Voices from *Church History*

"Work is permeated with purpose; it is intended to serve God, benefit humankind, and make nature subservient to the moral program of creation… Therefore we apply our whole being—heart and mind, as well as hand—to the daily job. As God's fellow workers, we reflect God's creative activity on Monday no less than on Sunday."[2]
  –Carl F. H. Henry (1913-2003)

Have you noticed the common thread in TV crime shows? Usually the suspense builds as the investigation comes to a standstill. But then the investigators figure out something game-changing by taking another pass through the crime scene or revisiting an old, dusty file from the archives. Part of the appeal of these programs is that the answer is there the whole time. That one earth-shattering piece of evidence is screaming out to everyone, trying to be noticed, yet everyone seems blind and deaf to it.

What if you lived in an environment in which someone intentionally left clues to tell you information about who he is and what he is like—and he actually wanted to be found? What if there were someone who wanted you to know him so much that he made an environment with the purpose of teaching you *about* him in order to lead to a relationship *with* him? And what if the depths of your heart rejoiced in new, unimaginable ways every time you learned something new about this amazing person because of the magnitude of who he was?

This is exactly what we see happen in the opening chapters of Genesis. God makes Himself known to us through the evidence of His being and the clues of His character that are sown into nature.

Here we will see that the creation of our world reveals the power and authority of God. Human beings are created in the image of God, and human relationships shine light on the nature of God. Because the Creator is sovereign, transcendent, and has chosen to personally reveal Himself to us, we are called to reflect His glory in our work and in our relationships.

God has all power and authority over His creation (Gen. 1:1-5).

To understand better what creation can tell us about God, we should look first to the way creation came into existence.

1 *In the beginning God created the heavens and the earth.*
2 *Now the earth was formless and empty, darkness covered the surface of the watery depths, and the Spirit of God was hovering over the surface of the waters.*
3 *Then God said, "Let there be light," and there was light.* 4 *God saw that the light was good, and God separated the light from the darkness.* 5 *God called the light "day," and He called the darkness "night." Evening came and then morning: the first day.*

There was nothing. Imagine that for a moment. The only mentionable presence other than God we see after the beginning was darkness. Formless. Void. Let that reality steep in your mind for a moment. Deadness. Emptiness. Lifelessness. That was the state before God continued.

Then for the first time in created history, God spoke. With the exercise of only His voice, God called forth light out of nothing, and light appeared.

God's transcendence, power, and authority are what commanded creation into existence. The very name used to describe Him in the account of creation above is *Elohim*, the common name of God in Hebrew that means mighty, powerful, and exceedingly great. It is the name that describes the kind of God who speaks and the universe is born, the name to describe a God who owns everything in creation because He spoke it into being. He is high, seated on the throne of the heavens that He spoke into existence. All created beings, including mankind, owe their allegiance to this amazing God because there is none like Him; there is no other God who has such power and authority, such bigness and transcendence.

At the same time we see the author of Genesis take a moment to retell the story of creation again in chapter 2, this time with a subtle yet critical difference. In the second account we see Moses refer to God as "Lord God." This name is different from the first. This name is the personal name of God; it doesn't describe an attribute or role of God but instead calls Him by His personal name: *Yahweh*.

When Moses uses the personal name of God, he is communicating something about Him. While we see God as powerful and authoritative in Genesis 1, we see that in the same process of creating, God is personal and intimate in Genesis 2. While He is separate and holy, He is also near and able to be known. And we don't just see Moses teach us that through His personal name. We see it in the very unique and intimate way God made man compared to the rest of creation.

He didn't just speak man into existence, though He absolutely could have as Elohim. Instead, God put His hands into the dirt and formed, shaped, and knitted man together with his fingers. And if that wasn't intimate enough, the Almighty lowered His head to the ground and met us face to face and breathed life into us. Can you imagine Adam's lungs inflating for the first time with the very breath of God giving him life? Do you see how intimate and close this Yahweh is as described in chapter 2?

It is true that as Elohim, God owns everything. All allegiance and worship is due Him because He is powerful and holy, set apart from all creation as the infinitely mighty Creator. He has rights over us, and we are accountable to Him. But there is this amazing truth we miss so often because our view of Him stops there. Yes, because He is Elohim, we *have* to give Him our all. But because He is Yahweh, the God who is near and compassionate with His people, we should *want* to give Him our all. We should *want* to surrender all of our rights because this kind of God wants better things for us than we could ever dream up for ourselves!

Because our God is Elohim, we *must* give Him all our worship, but because He's Yahweh, we *gladly* offer it, as nothing else could make us happier.

The clearest place you see the greatness and closeness of God is in the Person of Jesus Christ. Even in the story of creation, we see Jesus play an active role. According to John 1, all things were made through the power and authority of Jesus Christ—the Word of God. And the same Word would later put on flesh and come to dwell with sinful man and would pay the highest price to see us reconciled to the Father. The Word who was present from the beginning and who will return at the end is Jesus. This is the One through whom all of creation was made and the One for whom all of creation exists.

God desires to be glorified by human beings (Gen. 1:26–2:3).

We've seen that one of the major purposes of Genesis 1 and 2 is to teach us something about God's nature. He wants to tell us who He is. But He doesn't stop there. He not only wants us to better understand His nature, He wants us to better understand our own nature, namely that we are made in His image. In the creation account, there is a special place given to the creation of human beings.

26 *Then God said, "Let Us make man in Our image, according to Our likeness. They will rule the fish of the sea, the birds of the sky, the livestock, all the earth, and the creatures that crawl on the earth."*

27 *So God created man in His own image;*
He created him in the image of God;
He created them male and female.

28 *God blessed them, and God said to them, "Be fruitful, multiply, fill the earth, and subdue it. Rule the fish of the sea, the birds of the sky, and every creature that crawls on the earth."* 29 *God also said, "Look, I have given you every seed-bearing plant on the surface of the entire earth and every tree whose fruit contains seed. This food will be for you,* 30 *for all the wildlife of the earth, for every bird of the sky, and for every creature that crawls on the earth—everything having the breath of life in it. I have given every green plant for food." And it was so.* 31 *God saw all that He had made, and it was very good. Evening came and then morning: the sixth day.*

2:1 *So the heavens and the earth and everything in them were completed.*
2 *By the seventh day God completed His work that He had done, and He rested on the seventh day from all His work that He had done.* 3 *God blessed the seventh day and declared it holy, for on it He rested from His work of creation.*

In the language of Genesis 1, we see creation coming into being simply because "God said." God said this and God said that and it was so.

It's almost as if God pauses, almost as if He stops to contemplate and deliberate before He creates man. It's noticeably different, isn't it? He doesn't say, "Let there be man!" He converses within the Trinity and decides to do something with man that has not been done with the rest of creation. There will be something uniquely glorious about man, making him the pinnacle of all God's handiwork.

We are the only creation of God made in His image. That is what God is showing us about our nature; it is defined by the fact that we bear His image.

God gifts parents in a special way to further understand this concept of image-bearing. See, there are a lot of things that are mine, but none are like my children. Unlike my house, my car, and my big screen LCD TV, I myself am bound up into their very physical and spiritual makeup. And because of that, they have access to parts of my heart that no one else and nothing else will ever have access to.

What practically does being made in the image of God include? Look again at the text. From this passage we see that the "image of God" refers to how we relate (v. 27), rule (v. 28), work (vv. 29-30), and rest (1:31–2:3).

Relate: We see something passed on to man through God's decision to make them male *and* female, to keep Adam from being alone. In creating different persons within "man," God is re-creating within humanity the same sort of structure that has existed within the Trinity for all of eternity. There is a community between the three Persons of the one God. The complementary nature designed for man and woman to display in creation is also seen within the fellowship of the Godhead. In this we see God inviting us to reflect His personal and relational nature by making us in His image.

Rule: When God determines that He is going to make man in His own image, the first thing He attaches to that new kind of creation is the capacity and responsibility to rule. All throughout the creation narrative, we have observed God demonstrate His power and dominion over all that He has made, right? And now we see God entrust some of that power and rule to mankind. He is allowing man to share in who He is by passing that authority on through His image.

Work: This one can be surprising. There are many people who think work was a result of the fall of man. But here in Genesis 1 and 2 we see God give the command to Adam and Eve to work. Essentially He makes them gardeners. He is commanding that Adam and Eve properly steward and tend to what God has created in order to make it flourish.

Rest: Lastly we see God pass the concept of rest down to man by sharing His image with him. This is a beautiful and blessed thing. God didn't rest because He was exhausted and needed a break—we know that from other places in Scripture. He's God. He did not rest because He was tired or worn out. But He knows that after working, we will be.

In the command for us to rest, He's showing us again what it means to bear His image. He's showing us that even though we are unlike any other creature in that we are most "like" God, make no mistake, we are not God. There is an unbridgeable difference between us and God. One of the most critical ways we can image Him to the world is by showing that we are not God.

See, He knows something about us. We have a tendency to try and take His place and act like Him. We have a bent to want to take Him off His throne, even in the most unintentional of ways. And so He wove into the fabric of creation the rhythm of work and rest that must be obeyed if we are to flourish. He has even designed that we sleep a third of our lives away to show us that we're not God. A third of our lives we lay unconscious, accomplishing nothing but a symphony of snoring, all the while testifying that we're not God. And that's our nature. Our purpose is to reflect God, to show God to the world without making ourselves out to be God.

While we have been given the honor and privilege above all other created beings to share the image of God and bear it to the rest of the world, we fall terribly short most of the time, don't we? It can get discouraging when we are confronted with our shortcomings if we are supposed to be the best at this, right? If only we evangelized better. If only we didn't mess up so much. How is there any hope if we, out of all of creation, are to image God and let the rest of the world see fully who He is?

Colossians 1:15 tells us that Jesus is the "image of the invisible God." He is the perfect image bearer. In every way that we fall short, Jesus displays God perfectly and fully. There is no deficiency in His image. There is no distortion or mar. He is the perfect representation of man displaying God in creation. He does what we were meant to do but never could because of sin, and because of Jesus' sacrifice on the cross, God looks at us as if we represented Him on earth just like Jesus did. We get the reward of perfectly reflecting God in the world while Jesus took the penalty we were owed for trampling upon God's image. Jesus fulfilled all that was lacking in our ability to image God to the world.

God reveals His nature through the creation of human relationships (Gen. 2:18-25).

Throughout this story, we have seen God make everything in creation; after each new thing, He steps back and affirms that it is good. With the emergence of mankind, He declares that the creation is *very* good. But out of everything that was good, there was something that He declared *not* good.

18 *Then the* LORD *God said, "It is not good for the man to be alone. I will make a helper as his complement."* 19 *So the* LORD *God formed out of the ground every wild animal and every bird of the sky, and brought each to the man to see what he would call it. And whatever the man called a living creature, that was its name.* 20 *The man gave names to all the livestock, to the birds of the sky, and to every wild animal; but for the man no helper was found as his complement.* 21 *So the* LORD *God caused a deep sleep to come over the man, and he slept. God took one of his ribs and closed the flesh at that place.* 22 *Then the* LORD *God made the rib He had taken from the man into a woman and brought her to the man.* 23 *And the man said:*

This one, at last, is bone of my bone
and flesh of my flesh;
this one will be called "woman,"
for she was taken from man.

24 *This is why a man leaves his father and mother and bonds with his wife, and they become one flesh.* 25 *Both the man and his wife were naked, yet felt no shame.*

What happened? There was something missing from the creation of man when it was just Adam. His aloneness and isolation was not right; it wasn't good. In fact, it didn't rightly represent God. Do you remember the personal part of His nature that was passed through the sharing of His image? There was a relational component to His nature that was shared in the making of man as male *and* female.

We touched on the male and female relationship a little earlier and would do well to revisit it again since this can be a controversial issue, even in the church. The distinct roles between the different sexes have long led to debate and frustration, but what we know for certain is that there is something important to God in the fact that He created them male *and* female; otherwise He would have stopped after creating Adam (that would've been bad on multiple levels).

The topic of men's and women's roles matters not because there is an argument to be won but because it has something to teach us about God. Both men and women are needed to rightly reflect God because just as the completeness of the Godhead exists within the community of the Trinity, the completeness of man could not be expressed in Adam alone apart from community.

The implications don't stop there; the marital relationship between men and women exists to demonstrate something about Jesus as well. Both men and women in a marriage relationship are called to display the Person of Jesus to this world.

Ephesians 5:22-33 teaches that husbands and wives put on display the beauty of God and the gospel of Jesus Christ in the way we relate to one another. In both instances of this calling, for males and females, the way to show Christ to the world goes against everything the world teaches about marriage relationships.

For husbands, instead of leading within the marriage through dominance and overpowering, you are called to serve, sacrifice, and give yourself up as Christ did for the church. Husbands, in the way that you lead your wife, you are saying something to the world about how Jesus leads the church.

For wives, though you are equal in dignity and personhood with your husband, there is a call on your life to lay down your rights and submit to your husband's leadership. This is such a countercultural worldview, isn't it? Yet it's exactly what we see in the gospel; it is exactly the example we have in Christ (see Phil 2:5-8).

Jesus was absolutely equal in personhood and dignity with the Father, but He didn't grasp this right with a clenched fist. Instead, He laid it down and submitted to the Father, even at great cost to Himself. The marriage relationship is such a unique and special calling. God has created the special place of marriage so that the world will see Him accurately, through the roles of both husbands and wives.

Conclusion

God designed creation to reflect His character and nature. There are clues everywhere about Him because He wants to make Himself known. From the twinkling stars to the vast oceans, breathtaking mountains, and image-bearing man—He is telling His story and displaying Himself for all to see.

Truly there is no God like ours. He speaks and the heavens obey. Day and night, all of creation sings of His glory and majesty. May we, as His image bearers, the most equipped to represent God in this world, join with the rest of creation in bringing glory to the Father who allows us to know Him. May we look forward to the day when we will know Him fully as He is, face to face, in the light of His glory that illuminates all of heaven.

Devotions

GOOD GIFTS FROM A GOOD FATHER

I remember when my wife, Angela, first showed me on that magic stick that we were pregnant with our first son, Malachi. There was a strange combination of excitement and urgency. I don't think that I could have been more excited, yet at the same time, I knew there was a lot to get done before we would be ready for the little guy to get here. We needed to make a place for him. He needed a crib; he needed clothes and diapers; he needed bottles and pacifiers—and my wife was like a walking nine-month countdown clock. Before we could welcome this new member of our family into the world, we needed to prepare for him, to have everything in place to provide for his every need.

Read the creation story in Genesis 1 and 2 very carefully. You'll notice that the author (Moses) paints a very similar picture, doesn't he? As God's work of creation took place, He knew that the pinnacle of His handiwork was going to be man. Humans are the final crown of creation. The creation story builds to the climax when God finally breathes life into the lungs of mankind for the first time. And once man is alive, God looks at him and points to everything that He has been preparing and creating and ultimately says, "This world is all for you! I love you! Enjoy this, and let Me meet your every need through all that I have provided for you!"

Your Heavenly Father has brought forth an entire world to point you to Himself.

Pause and Reflect

1   Have you considered that God hung the stars knowing they would point you to His glory?

---

2   When you think about God, do you see Him as a loving and lavishly giving Father? Do you see yourself as His child and a receiver of His great affection?

---

3   What might be some things that prevent you from seeing God in this way?

The Blessing of Work

In this chapter we learn a little bit about the biblical view of work. Within the western culture that we live in, work is often the most defining identity of a person, even for people who are Christians. My guess is that happens because it is easy for us to feel strongly connected to the things we do, and work is a big part of how we spend our weeks.

Based on the way most people talk about their jobs, you would expect most churchgoing people to tell you that work is a result of the fall of man. I remember thinking that for a long time myself. Man sinned, and then God cursed him with work. That empowers every accountant glued to a computer during the months leading up to April 15 to shake his head and then his fist at Adam and Eve for bringing this evil upon the rest of mankind.

But what if we have a wrong view of work? What if our view of labor is influenced by the fact that we fell and not because work is fallen in and of itself?

Consider what it would be like if work was actually a testament of our being created in the image of God. Perhaps the intent and purpose of work is bigger than anything you ever imagined when you interviewed for the position you have today.

Pause and Reflect

1   What do you think it is about work that causes so many people to see it as a punishment?

----

2   How do you think work could help us represent God and show Him to the world?

----

3   Ask God to soften your heart to what the Bible says about work and life.

BREATHING LIFE TODAY

Knowing God is the highest joy and satisfaction that any human can experience. It is the very thing we were created to experience. He commands us to do everything we do for His glory (1 Cor. 10:31). But the good news is that when we glorify God, we find our greatest satisfaction and a sense of purpose because that is precisely what we were created to do.

How should this truth affect the way we live?

There are billions of people in the world who have never experienced the joy of doing what they were created to do. They are like birds that have never felt the freedom of flight; they are sitting next to you at your workplace, mowing the lawn next to yours, and sharing the city that you live in. They are lost and looking for something to save them or have already settled on being their own savior. Our hearts ought to feel compassion for those around us. It wasn't too long ago that we were in the same boat.

But if it is true that our God is real and wants to be known, if it is true that He is both all-powerful and intimately tender with His people, if He is worthy of all our praise and He is the One we most want to give our praise to—then we should want to be on mission with Him doing the things that He is doing!

God is on the move, breathing life into His creation once again by calling people to salvation—and this time we are invited to come along. The question is: Will we follow?

Pause and Reflect

1   How does seeing God as He reveals Himself in the Bible motivate your heart to talk about Him with people who do not know Him?

----

2   What are some things that hold you back from sharing Him with others?

----

3   How does the promise that God does not love you less, even as you struggle to understand His mission, encourage you to press on?

DISCUSSION QUESTIONS

1   What does the emergence of light tell you about God? What clues about Him are woven into that act of creation, the manner in which He made light?

2   Can you think of some reasons Moses would want to give us two perspectives on the same creation story by referring to God in two distinct ways? What do you think he is trying to tell us about God?

3   Is there anywhere else besides at the creation that we see the transcendence of God and His nearness displayed so clearly at the same time? Can you think of a time in your life when His power and authority met with His gentleness and closeness?

4   When it comes to the creation of man, what does God say? What is different about how God decides to create man?

5   How does it impact you to think of the God who made the heavens and the earth choosing to make you in His image? What does that tell you about the way He feels about you specifically?

6   In what ways do you image God best? In other words, in what area of your life (relate, rule, work, rest) do you feel most confident that you reflect God?

7   In what area do you feel you're the weakest, and why do you think that is your weak area of bearing the image of God? What are some practical ways you can improve?

8   In what ways does the truth about the image of God affect the way we treat others?

9   How does the recognition that work is assigned by God change our perspective on our jobs?

10 What does the picture of Eden teach us about sexuality and marriage? In what ways can we evaluate our marriages in light of God's original intention?

Chapter 2

The Fall

Paradise Lost and the Aftermath

Not long ago, I was watching Disney's *Beauty and the Beast* with my daughter. The story begins with a handsome prince who lives in a castle. When the prince turns away an old lady needing shelter, the old lady reveals herself as an enchantress. She curses the prince for his lack of hospitality, turns him into a hideous beast, and transforms his entire household staff into inanimate objects, such as teapots, clocks, and candelabras.

Up until now, whenever I've watched *Beauty and the Beast,* I've sided with the enchantress. After all, the prince needed a major attitude adjustment! But during the most recent viewing, I felt like the prince got dealt a tough hand. Was it really necessary that he should be turned into a horrible monster and forced to be a prisoner in his own isolated home buried deep in the woods? And what of his household staff? They didn't turn the lady away, and yet they were all affected by his actions. I began to think the enchantress's curse was a huge overreaction. Why all of this fallout over something that seemed so small?

Then it hit me. Deep down, many people see God's reaction to Adam and Eve's sin in the garden of Eden in much the same way. Sure, God said we shouldn't eat the fruit and we went against Him, but has all the pain and terror that followed that decision really been necessary? Many people read the story of Adam and Eve and wonder if the punishment of death is just a cosmic overreaction. Wasn't there an easier way to teach Adam and Eve a lesson without taking us all down with them?

In this chapter we see that what happened in the garden was about more than just a piece of fruit. The same sin that occurred in that place thousands of years ago is still happening every single day in our hearts. The first humans rebelled against God's rightful authority, leading to God's just judgment upon the world. Though the image of God in man has been shattered, God is gracious, and He offers salvation that comes through judgment.

Humans reject God's authority (Gen. 3:1-7).

Previously we studied the beginning chapters of Genesis and saw that they portrayed two very important aspects of God: His majestic holiness and His tender love. The God we read about in Genesis has the power to speak the earth into existence as well as the tenderness to walk with people as they enjoyed what He had made.

In the garden of Eden, God had provided everything that Adam and Eve would ever need. His only prohibition for Adam and Eve was not to eat from a particular tree. This rule was not an arbitrary command. He told them not to eat from it because death would be the result of their disobedience.

God wanted Adam and Eve to believe Him for their good. But Satan—a mysterious figure who opposes God—slithered onto the scene in the form of the serpent. And the serpent planted a very serious and grave lie into the heart of Eve.

1 *Now the serpent was the most cunning of all the wild animals that the* L*ORD* *God had made. He said to the woman, "Did God really say, 'You can't eat from any tree in the garden'?"*

2 *The woman said to the serpent, "We may eat the fruit from the trees in the garden.* 3 *But about the fruit of the tree in the middle of the garden, God said, 'You must not eat it or touch it, or you will die.'"*

4 *"No! You will not die," the serpent said to the woman.* 5 *"In fact, God knows that when you eat it your eyes will be opened and you will be like God, knowing good and evil."* 6 *Then the woman saw that the tree was good for food and delightful to look at, and that it was desirable for obtaining wisdom. So she took some of its fruit and ate it; she also gave some to her husband, who was with her, and he ate it.* 7 *Then the eyes of both of them were opened, and they knew they were naked; so they sewed fig leaves together and made loincloths for themselves.*

Satan knew that if he wanted Eve to sin, he would need to make her doubt if she could really trust God. He convinced her that God was holding out on her. Satan put the idea in her mind that God wanted her to stay away from the tree not so she wouldn't die but because He didn't want her to truly live. All of this time, God had been the Person providing for her every need, but for the first time, she was confronted with the possibility that there might be more for her outside of God's will than within it.

Adam and Eve rebelled against God by eating the fruit. With this choice, our first parents plunged humanity into darkness. Their sinful choice was an act of rebellion against God's authority and His goodness.

Before the sin of Adam and Eve, God had been the Person who determined what was good and bad in creation. When they took that first bite, the first humans declared that *they* were going to decide what was best for them. They didn't want God to tell them what they needed; He couldn't be trusted anymore, and it was no longer His place to decide. Instead, each person would determine his or her own course of action. In that moment, humans grasped for the authority that belonged to God as our Creator and took it for themselves. We decided to be our own gods.

Our disobedience didn't stop with the rejection of God's authority; we also belittled His goodness. Before sin, Adam and Eve believed that God wanted the best for them. A loving relationship existed between God and His image bearers.

After our rejection, humans no longer saw God as the near and intimate Father they had once known so well. We began to think that if we obeyed Him, we would miss out on something. Even today, many think of God as being out to sabotage our happiness and joy.

Our act of sin was not primarily about a piece of fruit. It was about the exchanging of God for an idol. In essence, with the eating of the forbidden fruit, we were saying to God, "Anyone or anything but You!" trusting even a crawling creature over the Creator.

What happened in the garden of Eden represents the exact same thing still happening in our hearts today. We don't believe God, but we're willing to believe anyone and anything else.

God judges those made in His image who fail to reflect His glory (Gen. 6:11-14,17-18).

I wish I could say the story gets more encouraging after this point. But we see just a few chapters later how sin was spiraling out of control. Things weren't getting better but much, much worse. Instead of one act of disobedience characterizing mankind, now "every scheme his mind thought of was nothing but evil all the time" (6:5). The author of Genesis tells us that God was grieved at the evil of humanity.

What we see from the grieving of God's heart is something very unique. God voluntarily (and that is an important distinction) bound His heart with man when He formed him with His hands. We didn't just get His image, we received His love and heartfelt affection. Consider the wonder of it all: The most powerful Being in the universe voluntarily bound His heart to man so intimately, with such intention, that when He sees our idolatry and rebelliousness, He experiences deep pain! Though we are about to see how God in His holiness must respond to sin and punish it severely, we can't pass too quickly over the grief that accompanies His righteous anger. Now let's look at an event that demonstrates God's judgment and mercy.

11 *Now the earth was corrupt in God's sight, and the earth was filled with wickedness.* 12 *God saw how corrupt the earth was, for every creature had corrupted its way on the earth.* 13 *Then God said to Noah, "I have decided to put an end to every creature, for the earth is filled with wickedness because of them; therefore I am going to destroy them along with the earth.*

14 *"Make yourself an ark of gopher wood. Make rooms in the ark, and cover it with pitch inside and outside.*

17 *"Understand that I am bringing a flood—floodwaters on the earth to destroy every creature under heaven with the breath of life in it. Everything on earth will die.* 18 *But I will establish My covenant with you, and you will enter the ark with your sons, your wife, and your sons' wives.*

We know from earlier in the chapter that Noah had found favor in the eyes of the Lord; that is why this covenant was extended to him. But notice that the covenant goes beyond Noah to benefit the members of his family. The righteousness of Noah was the foundation of the preservation of the rest of his family.

Does that sound like anyone else you know? The story of Noah points us ahead to Jesus. In Noah we see a pattern for how God is going to offer ultimate salvation. Jesus is the One in whom God was truly pleased, the One God truly favored. Though all have sinned and fallen short of the glory of God, though none are righteous, not even one, based upon the sole Person of Jesus and His righteousness, God offers us salvation.

Noah's family is saved not on the basis of their righteousness but on Noah's. They're saved because they belong to Noah. Likewise, we're not saved by our own works but by the work of Jesus alone, and we're saved if we belong to Jesus.

Through the story of the flood, we see the introduction to the gospel as salvation through judgment. What does this mean? While the entire world was looking up at God and rejecting Him—telling Him that they don't trust Him, just like their parents before them—Noah was building an ark. He was demonstrating with his life that he believed God. He had faith that God was going to do what He had said. And the waters of judgment did come.

Here's what I mean by "salvation through judgment": The same water that swallowed everyone who didn't believe in the word of God actually lifted Noah up. As the waters increased, everyone else was pressed down and crushed. But at the same time Noah and his family were lifted up and saved. The waters of judgment actually saved him; it was salvation through judgment. And Peter confirms this for us later in the Bible: "when God patiently waited in the days of Noah while an ark was being prepared. In it a few—that is, eight people—were saved *through* water" (1 Pet. 3:20, italics added).

Surprisingly, the waters were actually salvation for some and death for others. In the biblical story line, the reality of salvation through judgment will be seen most gloriously in the cross of Jesus Christ. As Jesus was judged on the cross for our sin, we were being saved. Salvation came to us through the very instrument by which death came to Jesus. God judges sin and wickedness, but He brings salvation out of this judgment.

Sin distorts human relationships that were intended to reflect God's character (Gen. 11:1-7).

We have seen that God judges sin and yet still pursues a restored relationship with sinners. But what about the broken relationships with one another? One of sin's consequences is the destruction of human relationships. The vertical rebellion (humans against God) leads to horizontal consequences (humans against humans). The first thing we see Adam do after God confronts him for his sin is point at Eve and blame her, right? All of a sudden, human relationships are a source of conflict and blame rather than help and harmony. Let's see how man attempts to address this problem by looking at a familiar passage centering on the Tower of Babel.

1 *At one time the whole earth had the same language and vocabulary.* 2 *As people migrated from the east, they found a valley in the land of Shinar and settled there.* 3 *They said to each other, "Come, let us make oven-fired bricks." They used brick for stone and asphalt for mortar.* 4 *And they said, "Come, let us build ourselves a city and a tower with its top in the sky. Let us make a name for ourselves; otherwise, we will be scattered over the face of the whole earth."*

5 *Then the LORD came down to look over the city and the tower that the men were building.* 6 *The LORD said, "If they have begun to do this as one people all having the same language, then nothing they plan to do will be impossible for them.* 7 *Come, let Us go down there and confuse their language so that they will not understand one another's speech."*

Do you see what is happening here? At the Tower of Babel, humans gathered around a common mission. They were united—one people. Their focus on a shared mission was actually bringing them together in such a way that God said nothing was impossible for them. This sounds great, right? A step in the right direction? Wrong.

The common mission that united the people at the Tower of Babel was the idea that they could make a great name for themselves. Unfortunately, they were unwilling to resound with the praises of God's great name. They were united in their rejection of God!

So we see God come down and *further* isolate mankind from one another by confusing their language. Their attempt to restore their relationships through their own mission actually made the situation much worse! Yet even here there is an element of mercy in this act of judgment. By confusing their languages, God slowed down the horrible developments that followed in the wake of human sinfulness.

Sin has affected everything. It has broken every relationship we have: with God, man, and creation. We need a better solution than Adam, but what hope do we have? We need a new and better "Adam." The Scripture teaches us that in Adam *all* sinned. You and I wouldn't have acted any differently if we had been in the garden with the serpent.

Yes, all of our individual acts of sin are very real and very serious. And yes, individual acts of sin qualify us as sinners, but our problem is even deeper than that. It is on the identity level, not just the action level.

Here is an example to help you see this truth more clearly. You can't tell this from reading my words, but I am Korean. I was born in Seoul, Korea. I don't just speak Korean, write Korean, and eat rice and kimchi with chopsticks; I don't just *do* Korean things. I *am* Korean. I'm Korean because my parents are Korean and their parents were Korean. Doing Korean things doesn't make me Korean, being Korean makes me Korean; it's an ontological issue.

And it is the same with our sin. We have a sinful nature because Adam is our head; our individual acts of sin contribute to our guilt before God. The only solution is a new head. Our old head brings death; we need a new head that will give us life. The good news of the gospel is that a new head has been offered to us in Christ Jesus (Rom. 5:17-19). God has adopted us through Jesus so that in the place of our sinfulness and judgment, He may grant us every spiritual blessing; through Him we are holy and blameless because that is the inheritance we receive under the headship of Jesus.

Did you sense your heart feeling that it's not fair when the Bible teaches us that we inherited a sin nature from Adam? Why should we receive the consequences for something we didn't do? But have we ever said that it's not fair when we hear the gospel, which says that we inherit a new nature from Jesus, that we receive the reward for something we didn't do?

The bad news is that we're not just sinners because we do bad things—it's deeper than that—we're sinners because we were born into Adam. But the good news of the gospel is that we can be good not through doing good things but by being born into Jesus, our new "Adam."

Through all of this, we see that God is bringing back the humanity that our sin has broken. He is restoring us to our created state as authentic humans who bear His image. Our relationship with God is remedied through Jesus. And our reconciliation with God also affects our relationships with other people.

When we repent and believe in Christ, we are forgiven and accepted by God. This truth must affect the way we treat others. When a brother or sister in Christ wrongs us and we desire to enact our own judgment against them, we are saying that the price Jesus paid for that sin on the cross was not enough. We are asking them to pay a little more because somewhere deep in our hearts, we believe the authority we hold as an offended party is greater than God's. Instead, we must freely offer forgiveness and pardon, just as we have been forgiven and pardoned.

The restoration of our relationship to God and our relationship to others means that the church is the inverse of Babel. We gather not to make a great name for ourselves but to make known the glorious name of Jesus Christ. We go out into the world on mission not to spread the news of our personal kingdoms but to spread the presence of the unfailing, never-ending kingdom of God.

Conclusion

Because of Jesus, God fully accepts us and treats us as if we are perfectly righteous, even though in practice we are not. In light of this grace that God extends toward us in Christ Jesus, we start treating others in the same way. For those who are in Christ, we accept others and love them even though in practice they fail us; we do so because in the same fashion, God accepts us and loves us even though in practice we fail Him.

God made a promise immediately after we sinned in the garden. He promised a way for us to be reconciled to Him, despite our dead hearts and deep rebellion. He wouldn't ignore sin and pretend it wasn't a big deal; it would be punished with the full fury of His infinite Being. Instead of aiming that fury toward the children He created, God aimed it at His eternal Son, who would buy us back at the cost of His precious blood.

We rebelled against God because we believed the lie that He could not be trusted, that He did not want us to truly live, that He wasn't good. But now through the sacrifice of His only Son, we see that He will stop at nothing to save us from the aftermath of that lie. In Jesus we see that God can be trusted and that He's not keeping anything from us; He gave His only Son to prove that. In Jesus we see that He's good and that He's more good than we could ever imagine.

Devotions

A Deep Truth

One of the most common things we heard growing up was the importance of being "good." There is a part of us that desperately wants to hear that we are "good." Maybe that is because deep down we know that we aren't—apart from Christ.

Romans 1:18-19: "For God's wrath is revealed from heaven against all godlessness and unrighteousness of people who by their unrighteousness suppress the truth, since what can be known about God is evident among them, because God has shown it to them."

Scripture teaches that people have an innate sense that there is a God whom they have offended; unfortunately, our heart suppresses this truth. We all know we are guilty, even if that feeling is so suppressed that we are oblivious to it.

There used to be a game show on television a few years back in which the player would be connected to a lie detector. To win the money, the player would have to answer a series of questions without lying. This got ugly fast.

One lady confessed to not loving her husband and having an affair—on national television. It seemed that nothing would keep her from the money. And then the last question: "Do you think you are a good person?"

She answered yes. We know from the deeply personal information that she shared that she was trying to win. When she answered yes, she was trying to tell the truth, but deep in her heart, she knew it wasn't right. And it registered as a lie.

Pause and Reflect

1   What does it say about our fallen nature that we are capable of suppressing such a grave offense against a holy God without even realizing it?

- -

2   What are some implications that follow from the truth that all people know there is something deep within them that isn't right?

THE ANSWER IS JESUS

There are so many definitions of sin, aren't there? I think one of the most common ones is "missing the mark." But that definition doesn't always translate into everyday life or convey the severity of what sin really is.

The main reason people sin is because we don't trust God. We don't really believe that He is going to provide, which is why we go out looking for things for ourselves. The definition of sin that we see from the garden of Eden is "not trusting God." That sounds more like my life than "missing the mark."

We grab for things because we think God is going to hold out on us. With our fists clenched around the things of this world, we scream, "How can I know? How can I truly trust that You are for me?"

God could look back at us in fury for doubting Him again. Who are we that we should demand God demonstrate anything? Yet we see Him answer this through the apostle Paul in Romans 8:32: "He did not even spare His own Son but offered Him up for us all; how will He not also with Him grant us everything?"

God's answer to our wandering hearts is found in Jesus. If He will not withhold His only Son to bring about our good, how much more can we be confident that He will give us all things that work together for our good?

Pause and Reflect

1   What are some areas of your life where it is hard to believe that God is for you?

2   How has God provided for you in the last week? Last month? Last year?

3   How can trusting God is for you help you fight sin more effectively?

GET IN THE GAME

One of the most challenging things about sin is fighting it. It can get weary and discouraging. Sometimes it can even feel like there is no hope. It is easy to start believing the lies that God can't use someone who struggles so much. We can start disqualifying ourselves and leaving the mission of God to people who have it more together.

Can you identify with that?

The fight against sin isn't just fighting the lies of sin before you sin but also fighting the lies of sin after you sin. And we must fight both well.

Christian, God has placed an incredible call and mission on your life, not because you are perfect but because Jesus was perfect. He knew what your struggles would be, and He made a way for you to have hope, not just before the failure but in the midst of failure and after the failure.

Philippians 1:6: "I am sure of this, that He who started a good work in you will carry it on to completion until the day of Christ Jesus."

Malachi 3:6: "Because I, Yahweh, have not changed, you descendants of Jacob have not been destroyed."

God made a promise and He will keep it. In Him you have all that you need for this fight, and through it you will be made stronger. And though our hearts are prone to wander and change, because He doesn't change, we will not be destroyed.

Pause and Reflect

1   How does God's faithfulness stir your heart to fight sin?

2   How does your perseverance resting in *God's* faithfulness rather than *your* faithfulness move you to worship?

3   Are there areas of God's mission in which you have put yourself on the sideline because of sin? How does the victory of Jesus over your sin encourage you to engage in His mission?

Discussion Questions

1   What do you think is the main reason why some people think God's punishment of Adam and Eve was excessive? What does that reason say about our view of God? Our view of ourselves?

2   What are the distorted beliefs that led Adam and Eve into sin?

3   Consider your own life and the choices you make. In what ways do we doubt God's goodness? In what ways are we also tempted to seek happiness outside of God?

4   How do God's love for His creation and His love for His glory lead to grief over our rebellion?

5   How does it impact you that God's heart was grieved by the sins of mankind? Does it surprise you that it brought about such an emotion in Him? What is the basis for this grief?

6   What does God's hatred of sin tell us about God's love for His glory and His love for creation?

7   How does the reality of judgment affect our sense of urgency in proclaiming the gospel?

8   Does the truth about original sin mess with your sense of justice? Why are we affected by the sin of another? How does the gospel message of Jesus paying for our sins challenge our view of what's fair?

9   What downward spiral of consequences have you experienced as a result of your own sin? What do these consequences tell us about God? About ourselves? About the nature of sin?

10 How can we show the world that we desire God's fame rather than the glory of our own names? How do our evangelistic efforts demonstrate our desire to make the name of God known to those around us?

Chapter 3

Abraham's Covenant

The Call of a Covenant-Keeping God

VOICES FROM *the Church*

"To Abraham, [God's] message was very moving. Literally. He told Abraham to follow Him to a place that He would show Abraham. God was establishing a people who would both hear His message and be His message unto all the world." [1]
–Jason C. Dukes

VOICES FROM *Church History*

"Wherever God in his providence guides you, let it be your joy to know that he is too wise to err—too good to be unkind." [2]
–Charles Spurgeon (1834-1892)

Everyone wants to be a part of something. That is why social media is so popular—we want to be connected. Remember kickball teams and birthday parties in school? People instinctively desire to have a team, home, a family.

The covenant family of God is the highest calling one can receive. Once we were invited into that family, but we threw it all away. Now we are born into the dysfunctional human family—which leads to death. We need a new family. We need God to make a way for us to be connected to *His* family again.

In this chapter we see how God initiated a rescue plan for His fallen creation that would ultimately bring salvation to sinners and display His grace. God called Abraham to be the father of a nation—a renewed humanity in covenant relationship with God. Like Abraham, Christians trust God's promises and are declared righteous before God.

God initiates a relationship with human beings (Gen. 12:1-4).

When God formed mankind with His own hands, it was the first time that God initiated a relationship with human beings. But as we will see from our next text, it wouldn't be the last. Watch how God laid the foundation for the family of God to be reunited.

1 *The LORD said to Abram:*
Go out from your land,
your relatives, and your father's house
to the land that I will show you.
2 *I will make you into a great nation,*
I will bless you, I will make your name great,
and you will be a blessing.
3 *I will bless those who bless you,*
I will curse those who treat you with contempt,
and all the peoples on earth will be blessed through you.
4 *So Abram went, as the LORD had told him, and Lot went with him.*
Abram was 75 years old when he left Haran.

God had a special calling for Abram. Right off the bat, God spoke to him, and not just any speaking, either. God spoke a blessing over Abram through promises. He told Abram some very specific things about how He would bless him.

First, God promised to make Abram into a great nation, meaning he would represent an entire line of people. Then He promised to give Abram a great name and a new land. Finally, God told Abram that all of the peoples on the earth would be blessed through him. Can you imagine hearing such promises from God?

To Abram these promises must have seemed extravagant and unlikely. His wife was barren. How could he be the father of a great nation if he could not produce one son? How could his name be great on the earth if there were no son to carry it on after he died? Up to this point in his life, Abram had never owned a piece of land. How could he come to have this promised land that God spoke of?

It's interesting to note how these promises to Abram are connected to the very things that suffer under the weight of human sin. In the previous chapters of Genesis, we've seen how sin has spread from generation to generation. The people who descended from Adam were born with the same evil, dark hearts that were displayed in the garden of Eden. At the Tower of Babel, people sought to regain a great name for themselves, but they went about it in a way that resulted in further condemnation. Even the land that was meant to serve humans was cursed after the fall, resulting in the toil and pain of mankind to produce anything from the ground.

But God is now addressing each of these problems through the promises to Abram. A new land is promised. Worldwide blessing is envisioned. New hearts will be given to people. God is now rolling out the plan of how He is going to restore everything that was lost in the garden of Eden. All of the consequences that stem from our sinful choices are going to be completely restored by God Himself.

Watch how Abram responded to this blessing and promise from God. He obeyed. Imagine for a moment that you are in Abram's shoes. God has come to you and made a number of grand promises that seem to be impossible based on your circumstances. Furthermore, this God is asking you to leave behind everything and go to a place you don't even know—a place that He will show you when the time is right.

In the same way that we saw God overcome the lifelessness and void that existed before the world was made, God took the lifeless heart of Abram and in grace called Abram to believe in the promises. In Genesis 1–2, God initiated a relationship with man by first creating Adam and Eve and then revealing Himself to them. Now in Genesis 12, we see God initiate the relationship once again. God comes to rebellious humanity through the covenant with Abram, and He again opens the door for relationship. God is the pursuer and initiator of the connection between Himself and man. He calls us to faith with the same voice that spoke light into darkness when He created the world from nothing.

Abram wasn't perfect. He didn't earn the right to have faith from God by being intelligent, charming, or even godly. Abram had faith because of God's gracious promises. And that is our story too.

Today, if we are putting our trust in Christ, we can't take the credit. God is the One who loved us and gave Himself for us. In 2 Corinthians 4:6, the apostle Paul makes clear: "For God who said, 'Let light shine out of darkness' has shone in our hearts to give the light of the knowledge of God's glory in the face of Jesus Christ."

The faith Abram demonstrated was a belief that God would bring him a son who would fulfill all the promises He made. In fact, without a son, all the other promises wouldn't matter. A great name would die if there were no son to carry it on. Land would be irrelevant if there were no son to leave it to when Abram died. How could there be a nation to come after him if there were not even one son? All of the promises of God hinged upon the promise of a son to Abram. The promise of a son was the centerpiece of all God's promises.

But Abram's faith was not only in the son who would be born to him; it was also in the Son who would be born through this nation of faith—the Son who would become the ultimate blessing. Abram looked ahead to the Son who would fulfill the promise of Genesis 3 to conquer sin and death forever—Jesus Christ.

God commands us to trust that He will keep His promises (Gen. 15:1-6).

As we turn to Genesis 15, we need to remember that years have passed since God first made His promise to Abram. They were some eventful years too. Abram almost lost his wife to Pharaoh. He almost lost the promised land to his nephew Lot. He almost lost his life and all his possessions in a war with four kings. He still had no child, and his current heir was a Syrian slave. We listen as Abram cries out to God in this reality—the gap between the promise and the fulfillment.

1 *After these events, the word of the LORD came to Abram in a vision:*
Do not be afraid, Abram.
I am your shield; your reward will be very great.
2 *But Abram said, "Lord GOD, what can You give me, since I am childless and the heir of my house is Eliezer of Damascus?"* 3 *Abram continued, "Look, You have given me no offspring, so a slave born in my house will be my heir."*
4 *Now the word of the LORD came to him: "This one will not be your heir; instead, one who comes from your own body will be your heir."* 5 *He took him outside and said, "Look at the sky and count the stars, if you are able to count them." Then He said to him, "Your offspring will be that numerous."*
6 *Abram believed the LORD, and He credited it to him as righteousness.*

Look closely at Abram's conversation with God. Can you discern his attitude? It seems as though Abram had little hope God would actually fulfill His promises. Fear and worry were starting to creep into his heart.

Notice the response of Abram as God reminded him of the promise that still belonged to him. The Bible says that as he was reminded, Abram believed God. This concept was picked up by the New Testament writers too. We are declared righteous before God by our faith in Him. We are not saved by moral accomplishment or religious exercise but by hearing the promises of God and believing them. God looks at faith and credits it as righteousness.

As Paul says in Romans 4:18-22: "He believed, hoping against hope, so that he became the father of many nations according to what had been spoken: So will your descendants be. He considered his own body to be already dead (since he was about 100 years old) and also considered the deadness of Sarah's womb, without weakening in the faith. He did not waver in unbelief at God's promise but was strengthened in his faith and gave glory to God, because he was fully convinced that what He had promised He was also able to perform. Therefore, it was credited to him for righteousness."

Here we are shown a "resurrection" faith—the kind that results in life from death—when Abram looked at his own body and saw that no life would be possible from him. He saw that the only hope of producing life had to come from God acting in his life, making something possible that was impossible for Abram to accomplish on his own.

That is the essence of our faith too. We look at our lives and see that there is no possibility of life coming from us on our own. We contemplate our realities and are moved to see the need for a Savior. We are incapable of life without Someone to save us from ourselves. The faith that comes as we realize our need for God is the exact kind of faith we see in Abram. This is what characterizes "resurrection"—saving—faith.

But there is still that pesky gap, isn't there? We believe God, but when confronted with circumstances that cause us to wonder if God will really come through, we see that saving faith is not always perfect faith. Abram himself cried out to God a couple of verses later, immediately after God had just reminded him of the promise He would keep: "Lord GOD, how can I know that I will possess it?" After everything, Abram's heart is still saying "Yes, I believe You, but how will I *know* that You are going to come through?"

Saving faith brings righteousness, but it also has fears, doubts, and struggles; ultimately its only hope is God. That is exactly what we see from Abram, who lived in the great gap between promise and reality. And that is where we live too.

In that day, a covenant was made by two people passing through the cut-up pieces of animals arrayed on the ground, with this understanding: If one party broke the covenant, then may what happened to these animals happen to them as well. Both parties were on the hook and subject to the penalty if they broke their promise to the other.

Yet when God made the covenant with Abram in Genesis 15:17-21, we see something unique. Who passed between the animal pieces? Not Abram and God, but God *alone* passed through.

As Abram was wondering, "God, how can I know with 100 percent certainty that You are going to fulfill these things You have promised?" God answered by assuming the full risk of the covenant. He walked through the slaughtered animals as a sign of His faithfulness to Abram. In other words, if He didn't fulfill His promises, then let His holiness and perfection be chopped into pieces like the animals. God provided a reminder. In essence, God was letting Abram know that nothing would stand in the way of His faithfulness to him.

What about us? That sounds great for Abram that God came down and gave him that reminder, but what about those of us in the gap right now? We're tired. We feel like we are hanging on by a very thin thread. We know in our minds that God will keep His promises, but every day that passes in the gap seems to loosen our grip on that trust.

Can't God give us something, just as He did with Abram? If He would just give us something to help us remember that He is faithful, then maybe we could make it through. I don't see any flaming pots or cut-up animals around here, do you? How can we know, like Abram, that we will possess all of God's amazing promises?

God answered our question 2,000 years ago, not with the blood of bulls and goats but with the broken body and spilled blood of His only Son. We see that God did not keep the promises just to prevent Himself from becoming like the divided animals; instead, He went as far as becoming like a slaughtered animal so He could keep His promises, so we would know there is nothing He won't endure to remain faithful to His Word.

When you find yourself in the gap and starting to grow weary, remember the covenant. Let your heart be overwhelmed by the greater reminder—greater than smoking pots and goats—that God has put before you in His crucified Son so that you never have to wonder if He loves you and will come through.

God desires that His people be set apart for His glory (Gen. 17:1-14).

We have seen that God calls people to faith and that faith is sustained by the covenant-keeping God. Now we are left with a couple of questions: What is the purpose of having this great faith? What does it accomplish? Read Genesis 17:1-14.

1 *When Abram was 99 years old, the LORD appeared to him, saying, "I am God Almighty. Live in My presence and be blameless.* 2 *I will establish My covenant between Me and you, and I will multiply you greatly."*

3 *Then Abram fell facedown and God spoke with him:* 4 *"As for Me, My covenant is with you: you will become the father of many nations.* 5 *Your name will no longer be Abram, but your name will be Abraham, for I will make you the father of many nations.* 6 *I will make you extremely fruitful and will make nations and kings come from you.* 7 *I will keep My covenant between Me and you, and your future offspring throughout their generations, as an everlasting covenant to be your God and the God of your offspring after you.* 8 *And to you and your future offspring I will give the land where you are residing—all the land of Canaan—as an eternal possession, and I will be their God."*

9 *God also said to Abraham, "As for you, you and your offspring after you throughout their generations are to keep My covenant.* 10 *This is My covenant, which you are to keep, between Me and you and your offspring after you: Every one of your males must be circumcised.* 11 *You must circumcise the flesh of your foreskin to serve as a sign of the covenant between Me and you.* 12 *Throughout your generations, every male among you at eight days old is to be circumcised. This includes a slave born in your house and one purchased with money from any foreigner. The one who is not your offspring,* 13 *a slave born in your house, as well as one purchased with money, must be circumcised. My covenant will be marked in your flesh as an everlasting covenant.* 14 *If any male is not circumcised in the flesh of his foreskin, that man will be cut off from his people; he has broken My covenant."*

Notice a parallel from this text that aligns with Genesis 1. God promised to multiply the descendants of Abraham. That was the first command God gave to Adam and Eve—be fruitful and multiply. Here we see that God was going to take ownership of multiplying the descendants of Abraham. God's people were going to reflect His glory by fulfilling His original intention for humanity, and He was going to be the One to accomplish that through faith.

This new family that began with Abraham is entered not through birthright or nationality. The true descendants of Abraham are children of faith as he was—they are those who trust in the promises of God. That is the heart of membership in this covenant family.

We know from Genesis 12 that we are called to be a blessing to the nations. It is in Genesis 17 that we start to see how we are to be a blessing. We see from circumcision that there is a distinction between the people of God and the rest of the world. This was a physical symbol distinguishing the people of God from the people of the world. It was to be a physical representation of a spiritual reality. Circumcision creates a mark not normally visible to others. The nature of the sign suggests it was intended to focus attention on the importance of Abraham's offspring, the royal line through which blessing would come.

In order to truly be a blessing to the nations, the children of God must maintain their distinction from the world. We must not forget the spiritual reality that demands change and repentance from the ways of the world—a need to be conformed to something else.

We have something game-changing to offer the world by inviting them to be reconciled to God; this covenant family looks different. As the world sees the differences in the way we live and behave as a result of the work of God in our hearts, they are drawn to experience the same through relationship with God. By showing the world our oneness, by showing how we love one another, serve one another, forgive one another in a way that's different than the world—by being different—we bless the nations.

Conclusion

We've looked at how God's plan of redemption for the world moved forward. A call that went out to Abraham and began the covenant family leads today to your calling and mine. The church is the family we are invited into through the call of God on our lives.

The faith required for membership in this family is our response to His call, and that faith is sustained by our covenant-keeping God. Faith is not sustained by your work, merit, or faithfulness; it is sustained because of *Christ's*.

Through this family we are distinctly blessed by God and called to proclaim the blessing of salvation to the rest of the world. Because our Father keeps His promises and does not change, we can rest assured that this family will be ours for all eternity. Every promise will finally be fulfilled and the gap will finally and fully be closed.

Devotions

Laughing at Promises

One of the things we see in Scripture is how God made promises to Abraham. One of those promises was to bring him a son. When he heard the promise from God, Abraham believed God even though it all seemed crazy given his circumstances (he was old and his wife was barren). Abraham's was a response of faith.

His wife, Sarah, however, had a different response: "So she laughed to herself: 'After I have become shriveled up and my lord is old, will I have delight?'" (Gen. 18:12).

Why was her response different? What was more believable in that moment than the promise of God? Her circumstances.

Sometimes our challenging circumstances are the perfect backdrop for God to demonstrate His faithfulness. We would rather Him keep His promises to us in ways that are comfortable and predictable. When we see poor circumstances, we see obstacles to the promises, but that is not the case with God. He uses all of our circumstances (the good and the bad) to best display His ultimate faithfulness.

Later in the story of Sarah, we see her laugh again. But this time she is holding her newborn baby. This laugh wasn't one of skepticism; this time it was a laugh of awe, a laugh of wonder at how faithful her God was to her.

Pause and Reflect

1 Identify three promises made by God to you in the Bible.

- -

2 Do any of those promises cause you to doubt or laugh because they seem unlikely in your current circumstances?

- -

3 How does believing that God is sovereign over your circumstances help you trust that He will keep His promises even when it seems impossible?

Faith and God's Call

The Lord called Abraham and he responded in faith. In this chapter we see how God's call to Abraham was grounded in grace and how Abraham's response was connected to the great salvation that would come through Jesus Christ.

Why do you think God set up salvation like this? A wandering man called by God to be the father of a great nation. How odd! How unlikely! The apostle Paul shines light on this truth in his letter to the Corinthians:

"Brothers, consider your calling: Not many are wise from a human perspective, not many powerful, not many of noble birth. Instead, God has chosen what is foolish in the world to shame the wise, and God has chosen what is weak in the world to shame the strong. God has chosen what is insignificant and despised in the world—what is viewed as nothing—to bring to nothing what is viewed as something, so that no one can boast in His presence" (1 Cor. 1:26-29).

Paul makes it clear in this passage that God calls for our faith in a way that no human can boast in His presence. If you and I believe in the great gospel of Jesus Christ today, it is not because we are smarter or more sensitive to the gospel or more moral. We believe today because of God's grace shown to us when we responded in faith to the Creator's loving call.

Pause and Reflect

1   How does it make you feel that God called you to salvation when you were undeserving?

----

2   Do you find yourself trying harder to please God or devastated when you fail because you think He loves you less?

----

3   How does the grace of salvation lead you to worship God more?

Community Apologetic

Mark 1:17: "'Follow Me,' Jesus told them, 'and I will make you fish for people!'"

This is one of the verses that I first became acquainted with when I became a believer. The imagery that came with it was of me standing on the side of a river with a fishing pole waiting for the chance to save a lost person all by myself. Can you identify with that?

But when Jesus made this declaration to His first disciples, fishing was a completely different affair. It was something that happened with a group of men, not something that happened individually. They would labor and work together as a team to pull in large nets of fish.

When I began thinking through the implications of that image, it started to change the way I view mission and engaging lost people. It seems as though this is something that can be approached more effectively through the family of God, the community of believers, than through me by myself.

As people see the family of God interact and live out the principles of Scripture—loving one another and laying down our rights as we saw Jesus do when He came to earth—it provides an alternate way of life than what the world offers and advocates. Seeing the many changed lives that are empowered through the love of God can compel others more powerfully to want to be reconciled to God and be adopted into this great family.

Pause and Reflect

1   How have you viewed mission traditionally? As something that is better individually or as part of a team?

- -

2   What are the benefits of engaging the lost with other believers?

- -

3   Why is it important to remember the distinct nature of believers compared to the rest of the world when you are on mission? What makes that challenging?

DISCUSSION QUESTIONS

1   In what ways does the desire to have a restored relationship with God and others show itself in our attitudes and actions?

2   How does our adoption into God's family show us the greatness of God's grace?

3   Why is it often difficult for us to take God at His Word? What does our unbelief say about our view of God's character and power?

4   What do you think caused Abram to respond by following God? What made it possible for the most unnatural and unexpected response to flow from his life?

5   What are some ways that your heart is like Abram's heart, struggling with fear and worry? In what ways are you living in the gap between God's promise to you and its fulfillment?

6   How would you expect God to respond to Abram when he groans about living in the gap? What does God's kind response tell us about His character and grace?

7   How does knowing that God always remains faithful to His Word help us through seasons when our faith is weak?

8   In what ways can we as a body of believers demonstrate that the blessing of salvation is to be proclaimed and passed on, not hoarded and chained?

9   How do holiness and distinctiveness aid us in our mission?

10   In what ways is the covenant family inclusive and exclusive at the same time? What implications does this truth have for the life of the church?

Chapter 4

The Exodus

God Comes to the Rescue

VOICES FROM *the Church*

"The only way to free ourselves from the destructive influence of counterfeit gods is to turn back to the true one." [1]
–Tim Keller

VOICES FROM *Church History*

"By [Christ's] blood, after our doorposts have been smeared [with it], that is, by the sign of his cross, after our foreheads have been marked [with it], we are freed from the ruin of this world as though from the captivity or destruction in Egypt. And we effect a most salutary passing over when we pass over from the devil to Christ and from this tottering world to his most solidly established kingdom. And therefore we pass over to God who endures so that we may not pass over with the passing world." [2]
–Augustine (354-430)

My son loves superheroes. It doesn't take long after we get home for him to disappear upstairs only to return dressed as Spider-Man. There he is, all three feet of him covered in red and blue as he dangles upside down from the couch, monitoring the safety of our home for catastrophic accidents and various villains. There have even been times he has saved his younger sister from the throws of her tangled blanket as if she were actually tied to railroad tracks!

There is something about being a hero that resonates with us. We love the idea of rescue. You can see it any time there are large gatherings of people huddled around the television during a hostage situation or when someone is trapped in a mine or a well as time is running out. Everyone bands together and pulls for the rescue.

These stories are meaningful because in the depths of our hearts, we know we need to be rescued. Somewhere hidden layers and layers beneath our confidence and comfort, we fear that something is wrong. There is a problem we can't fix. Maybe if we really got deep enough into our hearts, we would see that we identify more with the person who needs to be rescued and less with the hero. Perhaps that is the design.

What if that story is woven into our hearts so that we might look upward, outside of ourselves, for help? What if all the smaller stories of rescue are really just shadows of the greatest rescue story ever told?

In this chapter, we will see how God demonstrated His faithfulness to His covenant people by rescuing them from captivity in Egypt. As God unleashed His judgment on Egypt, His people trusted in God's Word, and they were saved through the substitute of the Passover lamb. God's deliverance formed the basis for the new community of people tasked with bringing glory to God's name.

God delivers us from slavery to the Evil One (Ex. 6:2-9).

Let's take a quick journey through the rest of Genesis so we can see the setup for the exodus story. Remember that God first called Abraham and promised him a family. Hundreds of years later, Abraham's family had migrated to Egypt and had grown substantially, to the point the family numbered over a million people.

The Book of Exodus begins with a new Pharaoh in Egypt who saw the growing number of Israelites (or Hebrews) as a threat to the empire. So he forced the Israelites into slavery and oppressed them with heavy burdens. To slow down Israel's growth, Pharaoh also commanded that every male son born to a Hebrew should be killed.

Desperate to protect her baby from being slaughtered, one Hebrew mother hid her son in a basket that was discovered by a member of the Egyptian royal family.

The boy—Moses—was raised in the Pharaoh's household. Years later, God called Moses to the greatest task of his life. But strangely enough, He didn't call him at the height of his power and influence in Egypt. He came to Moses after he had been living in exile, working as a shepherd, 40 years after his days in the palace— not surrounded by loftiness but now by lowliness.

Moses had not been immersed in prestige for some time. He was in a place where he was exposed to something he would never have experienced in the royal palace: humility. That was the missing ingredient for Moses' leadership. It would have been hard for Moses to learn humility in the palace. God stripped all the luxury away in order to equip him for the work He would do through him.

2 *Then God spoke to Moses, telling him, "I am Yahweh.* 3 *I appeared to Abraham, Isaac, and Jacob as God Almighty, but I did not reveal My name Yahweh to them.* 4 *I also established My covenant with them to give them the land of Canaan, the land they lived in as foreigners.* 5 *Furthermore, I have heard the groaning of the Israelites, whom the Egyptians are forcing to work as slaves, and I have remembered My covenant.*

6 *"Therefore tell the Israelites: I am Yahweh, and I will deliver you from the forced labor of the Egyptians and free you from slavery to them. I will redeem you with an outstretched arm and great acts of judgment.* 7 *I will take you as My people, and I will be your God. You will know that I am Yahweh your God, who delivered you from the forced labor of the Egyptians.* 8 *I will bring you to the land that I swore to give to Abraham, Isaac, and Jacob, and I will give it to you as a possession. I am Yahweh."* 9 *Moses told this to the Israelites, but they did not listen to him because of their broken spirit and hard labor.*

God's plan was to rescue His people. And we see that He was not *just* going to rescue them so they would be free; He was rescuing them for a purpose. When we think of Moses, we think of the phrase "Let my people go!" But the passage above shows us that the plan was bigger than mere freedom. God was demanding that His people be freed *so they could worship Him.* He wasn't liberating them just so they wouldn't have to serve the Egyptians; instead, God liberated them so they could serve *Him.*

The modern view of freedom is that we should not have any lord at all. With this view of liberation, we are free to do whatever we want to do. We are the boss. We call the shots. The picture of God we see in Exodus challenges that perspective. True freedom doesn't come from having no lord at all but by submitting to God, the world's true Lord.

God carried out the process of rescuing His people through bringing a series of plagues upon Egypt after Pharaoh refused to release the Israelites. They started out smaller in magnitude and built as Pharaoh's heart continued to harden and resist the liberation of God's people. While some of the plagues were small in scale at the beginning, they were very intentional. When God turned the Nile River into blood and caused the sun to be darkened, He was specifically demonstrating His power over the Egyptian gods.

So on the one hand, we see God's judgment falling upon the Egyptians as the plagues came. But on the other hand, we see God's kind mercy toward the Israelites. Keep in mind that the Hebrews had been in slavery at this point for 400 years. Entire generations had been born and then died in servitude to the Egyptian people and under their cultural and spiritual influence.

Imagine the impact captivity had on their lives. The Israelites were supposed to be the children of promise; there was supposed to be protection and blessing for them—and yet they were slaves. The gods of the Egyptians seemed to be more attentive and responsive than the God of Abraham, Isaac, and Jacob. Surely there would have been a tendency to forget the supremacy of God. Surely their hearts were starting to bend to the gods that seemed to care for those who worshiped them.

But the true God was not asleep. He knew that His people would be slaves for 400 years. He had been actively setting the stage for their deliverance from the beginning. His faithfulness never wavered. Through the plagues, our covenant-keeping God demonstrated His power over the idols of Egypt and destroyed any temptation for His people to trust those idols. Through His judgment of Egypt, God was winning back the hearts of His people.

What a great promise of deliverance! But did you notice the last verse of the passage above? Moses delivered good news to God's people, "but they did not listen to him because of their broken spirit and hard labor." You see, even with the promise of freedom laid out for them, their broken spirits prevented them from believing. The good news was too good to be true.

For generations God's people had passed through the harsh and ruthless rule of the Egyptians, and though God's promise was everything they had yearned to hear, the Israelites had abandoned all hope. The oppression had reduced their faith to a mere flicker. It would take a great act of God to rekindle the flame of faith that once burned in the hearts of God's people. Thankfully, a great act was just what God had in mind.

God delivers us from the judgment we deserve (Ex. 12:5-13).

5 *You must have an unblemished animal, a year-old male; you may take it from either the sheep or the goats.* 6 *You are to keep it until the fourteenth day of this month; then the whole assembly of the community of Israel will slaughter the animals at twilight.* 7 *They must take some of the blood and put it on the two doorposts and the lintel of the houses where they eat them.* 8 *They are to eat the meat that night; they should eat it, roasted over the fire along with unleavened bread and bitter herbs.* 9 *Do not eat any of it raw or cooked in boiling water, but only roasted over fire—its head as well as its legs and inner organs.* 10 *Do not let any of it remain until morning; you must burn up any part of it that does remain before morning.* 11 *Here is how you must eat it: you must be dressed for travel, your sandals on your feet, and your staff in your hand. You are to eat it in a hurry; it is the LORD's Passover.*

12 *"I will pass through the land of Egypt on that night and strike every firstborn male in the land of Egypt, both man and beast. I am Yahweh; I will execute judgments against all the gods of Egypt.* 13 *The blood on the houses where you are staying will be a distinguishing mark for you; when I see the blood, I will pass over you. No plague will be among you to destroy you when I strike the land of Egypt.*

The tenth and final plague was different from the ones before it. The earlier plagues fell solely upon the Egyptians, their land, and their livestock. But regarding the final plague, no one in the land of Egypt was exempt. Egyptian and Israelite were equally susceptible to the coming judgment. The firstborn children in all the land would die.

Unless… There was a provision for salvation established by God, a way to be spared from the death accompanying this judgment, but only one way— salvation through a substitute.

From the text above, we see that God laid out a very specific substitute for the people of God to rely on for their salvation from the tenth plague. To be saved, Israel was called to act faithfully, to demonstrate that they were God's people by holding a Passover feast and spreading the blood of the Passover lamb on their doorposts. God's instructions stated that not just any lamb was acceptable; God demanded an unblemished lamb to serve as the substitute. The blood required for salvation was from a perfect lamb.

What a picture this is, and what a call to action for the Israelites! God was sounding the siren. Even the way He had them eat the feast communicated that He was on the move and getting ready to bring about their deliverance. They had to have their shoes on and their staff in hand; their bread wouldn't even have time to rise because of how fast they would break free from the slavery that had marked their entire lives. All of these elements surrounding the Passover feast were shrouded with the anticipation of promise-fulfillment.

This act of God positioned them in the posture of faith opposite the broken spirits Moses encountered in Exodus 6. This demonstration of power ignited the faith needed for the Israelites to believe God would finally rescue them from slavery. And that's just what God did.

God delivers us into a community designed to glorify His name (Ex. 14:10-14).

Once the Hebrews began their exodus from slavery, the hearts of the Egyptian leaders again became hard. They wanted their slaves back. They couldn't let them just walk away. So Pharaoh mounted an army and led them into the wilderness in hot pursuit of the Israelites.

Remember that the people of God were leaving Egypt primarily on foot and with their various animals. This wasn't a fast-paced race to the promised land. It was a walking caravan comprised of over a million men, women, and children. Though they had a head start, it wouldn't take long for the Egyptians to start closing in on them. Let's take a look at the text and see how God's people responded to the Egyptians chasing them:

10 *As Pharaoh approached, the Israelites looked up and saw the Egyptians coming after them. Then the Israelites were terrified and cried out to the LORD for help.* 11 *They said to Moses: "Is it because there are no graves in Egypt that you took us to die in the wilderness? What have you done to us by bringing us out of Egypt?* 12 *Isn't this what we told you in Egypt: Leave us alone so that we may serve the Egyptians? It would have been better for us to serve the Egyptians than to die in the wilderness."*

13 *But Moses said to the people, "Don't be afraid. Stand firm and see the LORD's salvation He will provide for you today; for the Egyptians you see today, you will never see again.* 14 *The LORD will fight for you; you must be quiet."*

What we learn from this text is that while we may be taken out of slavery in an instant, it takes much longer to take the slavery out of us. From the moment Pharaoh released them from Egypt, they were no longer slaves. Their identity had changed. It was over. And yet instead of looking forward to the promised land, they looked back toward their life in Egypt. Why in the world would they want to go back? After everything God had just shown them, how could they doubt?

When we trust in Jesus Christ, we are pulled out of slavery to sin. We are taken from the domain of darkness and placed into the kingdom of light. We are justified and declared legally innocent in the sight of God because the righteousness of Christ is credited to us. We are made sons and daughters—in just an instant.

But how often do we longingly look back on the days when we were slaves? How often do we find ourselves wishing we could go back because we had learned how to make slavery comfortable? Learning to live free is hard when all you know is how to be enslaved.

The behavior of the Israelites in this story is nothing to look down on or scoff at. It is a portrait that reveals our own hearts and exposes our tendency to reject God because we are so used to serving a different master. We are just like them—no better.

Moses handled the people's hysteria by commanding them not to be afraid and to know that the Lord would fight for them. Then as he stretched out his staff, God split the sea that was blocking the Israelites in, and Moses led his people through on dry land. Once the Hebrews were through to the other side, the waters fell. In a moment, Egypt's powerful army was wiped from the face of the earth. The great empire had fallen.

Surely the surrounding nations would hear of this! What great nation conquered the entire Egyptian army? It must have been an abundant, mighty army. The chariots and fighters must have overpowered the Egyptians in an unimaginable way, right? How surprised the nations must have been to hear that it was the God of the slaves! Think of the shock and awe that must have fallen on them to hear that the God of the Hebrews parted a sea for His people and then used the same sea to destroy their oppressors.

Through this act of deliverance, God demonstrated His faithfulness to the covenant He had established with Abraham hundreds of years before. The salvation of the Israelites allowed them to be a blessing by reflecting the glory of the true God to all the nations. *He* was the One who defeated the Egyptians.

The nature of this salvation was meant to showcase the glory of God to His chosen people and to all the peoples of the earth. He was the King who would fight for and defend them from their enemies. With their backs to the Red Sea and nowhere to go, God brought them to the very point where His glory would be displayed. All the Israelites were commanded to do was wait on Him.

Waiting is one of the defining characteristics of the people of God. We are a people who look to God and wait for Him to act on our behalf. The Red Sea would not be the last time we see the children of promise waiting. In fact, several generations later we see someone still waiting to see God's salvation. But this time the salvation would not be from the grips of the most powerful nation on the earth—it would be from the very wrath of God Himself.

Simeon was a righteous man who believed God. The Holy Spirit revealed that he would not see death until the Lord's Christ, our new and better Passover Lamb, was born. He had been waiting all his life to see the Lord's provision. More than a thousand years after Moses parted the Red Sea, Simeon watched as Joseph and Mary walked into the temple with Jesus in their arms. Simeon knew that God had been faithful to His promise, that He would again rescue His people from their slavery.

And once again we see that the salvation of the Lord brought blessing to the world. This blessing for Israel would serve as a blessing for the rest of the nations. In Christ there would be a light of revelation even to the Gentiles. God's rescue project would not be limited to only the Israelites. Christ's rescue this time was bigger. It was for people from every tribe, tongue, and nation who would be covered by the blood of this Substitute. This salvation would be eternal, not coming at the cost of one unblemished lamb but at the cost of God Himself.

Conclusion

The greatest heroes are the ones who give everything, including their lives, for the mission of saving others. These move our hearts most because there is nothing more to give, nothing withheld.

The story of the Passover points us forward to the cross—the place where God did not hold back anything to rescue us. He knew there was nothing we could do to save ourselves. God didn't ask someone else to take the fall; He didn't sacrifice His character of justice to reduce our guilt. God took the punishment for us. He sacrificed Himself so we would be saved.

There is no greater Hero. There is no better story. Heaven has nothing more valuable and complete than Jesus to offer. May we rejoice at the salvation of the Lord and begin worshiping Him now as we will forever in His kingdom.

Devotions

A New Kingdom

In the beginning, God was the intended and rightful ruler of our hearts as the Creator. When we fell in the garden of Eden, mankind initiated a change in leadership. We were banished from the kingdom of paradise and instead served a new master in the kingdom of darkness.

There was no way of escape. No force of human effort could change our placement in this new kingdom. Every subject in this kingdom shared the same fate of oppression and destruction at the hands of their new king.

The only hope of deliverance from this evil empire was a rescue mission. Not from an army or by a revolt of the people, this mission could only be accomplished by God Himself. He would cross enemy lines to save the heirs of His kingdom who were lost. This King wouldn't ask us to fight with Him to get out; He would trade places with us. Through this rescue we would be transferred back into His kingdom, and this time we would be sealed forever, unable to ever be removed from His rule again.

Colossians 1:13-14: "He has rescued us from the domain of darkness and transferred us into the kingdom of the Son He loves. We have redemption, the forgiveness of sins, in Him."

Pause and Reflect

1   Have you considered the kingdom you once served in before you were a believer? What lesser kings did you serve in the domain of darkness?

- -

2   Do you ever find yourself longingly looking back on the days of your slavery, forgetting the oppression you were under? What makes it hard to remember how horrific that kingdom truly was?

- -

3   What is your response to God as your rightful King?

For His Name's Sake

There can be a temptation to believe that God rescued us because we were worth it. In some sense, it is true that we are of great worth to God because of our being created in His image. At the same time, that worth serves not to end with us but to elevate God's glory with worship.

In fact, that is what we were made to do. We weren't made to point to ourselves and be moved with our own value. We were made to point to God and be moved with His value. We were created to be "spent," to declare His goodness to all of creation. Unfortunately, we abandoned our holy calling.

When God came for us, He was doing it out of love for us—because worshiping Him is where we will find our highest joy. But more than anything, He was coming for us because of His glory and name—to save worshipers for Himself who testify to the world that He is the one true God.

In Ezekiel, God talks about coming for His people, and He shares His motivation with them clearly:

"Therefore, say to the house of Israel: This is what the Lord God says: It is not for your sake that I will act, house of Israel, but for My holy name, which you profaned among the nations where you went. I will honor the holiness of My great name, which has been profaned among the nations—the name you have profaned among them. The nations will know that I am Yahweh" (Ezek. 36:22-23).

Pause and Reflect

1   How does it make you feel knowing that God is preserving His name by rescuing His people?

- -

2   How does putting yourself as the highest priority of God (higher than His glory) jeopardize the character of God?

- -

3   How can this view of God's concern for His own glory lead you to worship Him more?

ALL AUTHORITY

For many of us, being on mission can be scary. We think about sharing the gospel with the people we love and can almost panic because we think we are going to mess it up. We start believing things that aren't true to spare us from having to fully engage in the mission.

We start thinking we need to know more before we can really impact the kingdom. We think we need to care more or have stronger relationships before we can tell people about our King. Some of us may even think we need to meet physical needs before we can start jumping into conversations about God.

We can take ourselves out of the game on mental, emotional, and physical levels. We look at the mission and then at ourselves and see every reason to stay on the sidelines.

According to these verses, why should we engage in the mission?

Matthew 28:18-20: "Then Jesus came near and said to them, 'All authority has been given to Me in heaven and on earth. Go, therefore, and make disciples of all nations, baptizing them in the name of the Father and of the Son and of the Holy Spirit, teaching them to observe everything I have commanded you. And remember, I am with you always, to the end of the age.'"

Why engage in the mission? Because all authority belongs to our King. It isn't about us and our weakness. God is the more powerful King, and He will not fail because of our shortcomings—He will look all the more glorious because of them.

Pause and Reflect

1   How does it make you feel to know that God has *all* authority? How does that affect the way you see mission?

- -

2   What are the barriers for you to engage the lost?

DISCUSSION QUESTIONS

1   Imagine the switch of circumstance for God's people. One change in leadership (a new Pharaoh) took them from prosperity to devastation. When has there been a time like that in your own life? What emotions did you feel? How did your faith influence your reaction?

2   Have there been times in your life when God moved you out of your comfort zone and took you to difficult places to develop you? How has God shaped and empowered you even during times He seemed absent?

3   Are there things you are tempted to trust more than God for your safety, provision, and comfort because God seems distant?

4   In what ways does the biblical view of freedom differ from the world's? How is our mission as God's people influenced by seeing ourselves as freed to serve?

5   Can you identify with the pain and numbness of the Israelites? Do the great promises of the Bible ever fall on deaf ears as you pass through times of profound brokenness? How might God use our brokenness and neediness to prepare us for receiving good news?

6   What do you think God wanted to teach His people by sending a plague that would affect both Hebrews and Egyptians alike? How does God's action reveal to us the universality of human sinfulness and our need for a substitute?

7   In what ways does the truth of God's provision of a substitute stir up faith and repentance in the hearts of His people?

8   In what ways does the complaining of the Israelites point a mirror to our own hearts? How does the tug of slavery to sin still affect our hearts even after we are redeemed?

9   In what ways have you seen the power of God after a season of waiting for God to act? Why is it important that God's saving actions on our behalf demonstrate our weakness and His strength?

Chapter 5

The Law

God Gives the House Rules

VOICES FROM *Church History*

"We must exhibit simultaneously the holiness of God and the love of God. Anything else than this simultaneous exhibition presents a caricature of our God to the world rather than showing him forth."[1]
–Francis Schaeffer (1912-1984)

VOICES FROM *the Church*

"Nothing can stop a people who are trusting in the Word of God and living for the worship of God."[2]
–David Platt

Have you noticed how hard it is to reverse an opinion you've held for a long time? There once was a time when I felt an overwhelming disdain for working out. I felt like it was just something to get in the way of my comfort. It turns out that now I feel differently about working out. I see physical exercise as something important and good. It doesn't mean that it is any less hard or not a drain at times, but I missed the good side of working out because I was so fixated on the difficulty. It's funny but even though my opinion has changed, the components of "working out" have stayed the same. It is still hard and good for me at the same time. In many ways, this is true of the way we approach the law in the Old Testament. It is hard and good for us at the same time.

In this chapter, we will explore the truth that the God who loved His people enough to bring them out of slavery is the same God who graciously gave them the law that would govern their life together. In the law we see God's holy character and His desire to be glorified by all people. We also learn how our obedience is intended to spotlight God's love and holiness.

God's giving of the law is an act of grace (Ex. 34:1-9).

Many people think about the law and immediately get the image of a stern Father doling out rules to His people because He is on some sort of cosmic power trip. Some imagine God is just waiting for the moment they break a commandment so He can crack on them. But this is certainly not the image we see from the text.

1 The LORD said to Moses, *"Cut two stone tablets like the first ones, and I will write on them the words that were on the first tablets, which you broke.* 2 *Be prepared by morning. Come up Mount Sinai in the morning and stand before Me on the mountaintop.* 3 *No one may go up with you; in fact, no one must be seen anywhere on the mountain. Even the flocks and herds are not to graze in front of that mountain."*

4 *Moses cut two stone tablets like the first ones. He got up early in the morning, and taking the two stone tablets in his hand, he climbed Mount Sinai, just as the LORD had commanded him.*

5 *The LORD came down in a cloud, stood with him there, and proclaimed His name Yahweh.* 6 *Then the LORD passed in front of him and proclaimed: Yahweh—Yahweh is a compassionate and gracious God, slow to anger and rich in faithful love and truth,* 7 *maintaining faithful love to a thousand generations, forgiving wrongdoing, rebellion, and sin. But He will not leave the guilty unpunished, bringing the consequences of the fathers' wrongdoing on the children and grandchildren to the third and fourth generation.*

8 *Moses immediately bowed down to the ground and worshiped.* 9 *Then he said, "My Lord, if I have indeed found favor in Your sight, my Lord, please go with us. Even though this is a stiff-necked people, forgive our wrongdoing and sin, and accept us as Your own possession."*

It's important to note that this event took place *after* Moses had already gone up to speak with the Lord. The first time, when Moses came back down, the Israelites had already turned to serving a golden calf instead of the powerful God who had *just* delivered them from bondage.

In light of Israel's idolatry, we might expect to see a very angry, frustrated God who responds like this: "Haven't I just given this law to you? Before you could even make it back down the mountain, the people had already turned away from Me! What is the matter with you guys? What makes you think I am going to give the law again?"

Parents might find this scene all too familiar. How many times does a parent communicate a rule to a child (for the child's good, no less!) only to have the child disobey within moments? One response to disobedience is immediate punishment. But in this passage, God showed remarkable patience with His children, even as He instructed them again.

Furthermore, God reminded Moses of His name. Remember our earlier study on creation? There we saw that the name of Yahweh is distinct from God's other names recorded in the Scriptures. Yahweh is God's personal name, which means that this act of declaring His name was not arbitrary. It communicates something about His nature as a covenant-keeping God who will not compromise His promises even in the face of His people's blatant rebellion.

Notice what God says after His name. He describes Himself as gracious and compassionate and slow to anger. For many of us, it's hard to believe God can feel this way about us after we sin. But we are mistaken. God's heart is full of love for His people.

Think about the goodness and grace of God. He doesn't immediately give us what we deserve after we sin. We know this is true because you and I are still here breathing in air. If God gave us the punishment that we deserve immediately, then we would already be dead! God has demonstrated patience. He has shown compassion and mercy.

At the same time, there is another half to that proclamation. Verse 7 says, "He will not leave the guilty unpunished." Just as He must display mercy to remain faithful to His covenant, He must also punish the guilty. Otherwise He would compromise the justice of His character.

Put yourself in the position of someone needing justice. Imagine a person you love was brutally murdered. What if the criminal were apprehended only to be let go by a judge claiming to be "gracious and compassionate"? You would rightly be angered. After all, the judge's action would communicate that the death of your loved one was inconsequential. You would cry out for justice.

The same is true of all sin. Our sins are an affront to a God who is anything but inconsequential. God upholds the glory of His name through His perfect justice. But thankfully, He is compassionate too. He is compassionate *and* just. At different times and seasons we may want Him to be one or the other, but the truth is we need Him to be both all the time.

The good news is that God *is* both. On the top of the mountain that day with Moses, God revealed both parts of His character. But even then, His revelation was not complete. He had not yet fully demonstrated the depths of His mercy. Neither had He fully demonstrated the uprightness of His justice. At Mount Sinai we catch only a glimpse of the fullness of God. It would be later, on a mountain named Calvary, that we would see the ultimate and full display of God's mercy and judgment.

But notice that even a glimpse evoked worship from Moses. As God passed in front of him, Moses had no other response than to fall on his face and worship God. Moses' face shone with the glory of God, and he reflected that glory back to the Israelites when he came down from the mountain. There is no higher response when confronted with the character of God than to bow. God's grace is designed to produce worship. And it does.

The law is a reflection of God's holy character (Lev. 19:1-2; Deut. 6:4-5).

1 *The LORD spoke to Moses:* 2 *"Speak to the entire Israelite community and tell them: Be holy because I, Yahweh your God, am holy.*

We've discussed the aspects of God's character that include both mercy and justice. The law also shows us how these two components of God's character can be on display at the same time. The law makes it possible for a holy God to dwell among a sinful people by creating a standard for His holiness and providing a way for the people to be spared the punishment for their failure to meet that standard. Leviticus sets forth the terms of the covenant that will permit God's presence among a sinful people. Leviticus 17:11-12 reads: "For the life of a creature is in the blood, and I have appointed it to you to make atonement on the altar for your lives, since it is the lifeblood that makes atonement. Therefore I say to the Israelites: None of you and no foreigner who lives among you may eat blood."

This is the birth of the sacrificial system. The concept unveiled here is that a life is required when there is failure to keep the standard of the law. God does not ignore it or sweep it under the rug. A life is demanded to account for sin. The blood from that sacrifice is to be spilled on the altar to make atonement.

The sacrificial system was not unique; other gods demanded sacrifices as well. The difference with this holy sacrificial system was that it was not inaugurated out of fear or to turn God into a divine vending machine designed to reward people for various ritual practices. That was the case with other gods. Their sacrifices were demanded out of fear of punishment or to gain blessing and approval.

No, the heart behind the Old Testament sacrificial system was always different. Sacrifices were to be made from a heart of love for God. They were not a means to get something from Him or win approval from Him; the sacrifices were the heartfelt sign of God's people who believed in His promise to preserve His people. God is not interested in perfunctory obedience. He desires that we love Him fully.

> 4 *"Listen, Israel: The LORD our God, the LORD is One.* 5 *Love the LORD your God with all your heart, with all your soul, and with all your strength.*

According to Jesus, the Deuteronomy passage above serves as the greatest commandment in all the Scriptures. If that is the case, then we see that God is primarily concerned with our love for Him, not just our individual actions. The highest priority—the commandment we should seek to obey above all others— is to love God with every part of who we are.

The trouble is that no matter how good we are at keeping the law, we do not perfectly love God with every faculty. We don't consistently and constantly love Him with all of our hearts. We don't seek to love Him with all of our souls. We don't spend ourselves to love Him with all our strength. We give other, lesser things portions of our being that should be reserved for God.

Think about it. Even if we obeyed every single aspect of the law and its practices, could we say that all of the seconds of our lives were spent loving God fully with all that we are in our entirety? If not, then we are in violation of the foremost commandment of God. And if that is our reality, we deserve the greatest punishment. We need a solution. We need something—or Someone, to be more precise—to atone for our sin and failure. Thankfully, we can see the compassion of God's character in the way He deals with His children.

The law guides the people of God in reflecting His character (Num. 14:11-19).

After the law was given to the people and they arrived at the promised land, they were surprised to see that the land was inhabited by large and numerous people. Not just any people, these inhabitants were described as giants, fearsome and scary. When the people saw this, they became angry and rallied one another to raise up new leaders and return to the slavery in Egypt. The response from God, in light of this rejection and fear of the people after all His provision, was laced with anger.

At this point, it looked pretty grim for Israel. It looked like God had finally come to the end of His rope and was about to make this a "Game Over" situation for His people. Thankfully, God had already communicated something about His unchanging character to Moses. His Word had already dictated who He is and who He will always be. Because Moses had been given the law that taught him about the perfect nature of God, he had a response to stand on in the face of this dire scenario.

11 *The LORD said to Moses, "How long will these people despise Me? How long will they not trust in Me despite all the signs I have performed among them?* 12 *I will strike them with a plague and destroy them. Then I will make you into a greater and mightier nation than they are."*

13 *But Moses replied to the LORD, "The Egyptians will hear about it, for by Your strength You brought up this people from them.* 14 *They will tell it to the inhabitants of this land. They have heard that You, LORD, are among these people, how You, LORD, are seen face to face, how Your cloud stands over them, and how You go before them in a pillar of cloud by day and in a pillar of fire by night.* 15 *If You kill this people with a single blow, the nations that have heard of Your fame will declare,* 16 *'Since the LORD wasn't able to bring this people into the land He swore to give them, He has slaughtered them in the wilderness.'*

17 *"So now, may my Lord's power be magnified just as You have spoken:* 18 *The LORD is slow to anger and rich in faithful love, forgiving wrongdoing and rebellion. But He will not leave the guilty unpunished, bringing the consequences of the fathers' wrongdoing on the children to the third and fourth generation.* 19 *Please pardon the wrongdoing of this people, in keeping with the greatness of Your faithful love, just as You have forgiven them from Egypt until now."*

Notice what Moses did. He spoke back to God what He had already declared to be true about Himself. He used the law as a guide to reflect God's character back to Him, and more importantly, He believed what God said to be true about Himself, even in light of a bleak situation. God remained faithful because of His character, not because Moses made a great argument or because the people deserved to be spared. Israel was spared God's judgment because Moses believed God on behalf of the people. He believed God was exactly who He claimed to be through His word to him.

It can be easy to look down on the Israelites at times like this, can't it? The more we look at this people, the more I realize it is like holding a mirror up to myself. My life is full of failure and sinful choices. I have often failed to take God at His Word. I need someone like Moses who will believe God on my behalf.

Thankfully there is Someone who has always believed God perfectly. We need Someone to be found in our midst in the same way Moses was found in the midst of Israel. We need Someone to believe when we don't. We need Someone to believe on our behalf—as did our brothers and sisters in the wilderness. Jesus is that Someone.

The Lord shows great mercy. He doesn't wipe out the nation of Israel and start over like He mentioned earlier. He pardons them as Moses requested, but the mercy is not alone—it comes through judgment. He is faithful to His character both to demonstrate mercy and to be holy.

In response to Moses' pleading, God pardoned His people. But the mercy came through judgment. He showed mercy by not destroying them and by maintaining His promises to Abraham. But He judged them by informing the generation of doubters that they would not see the promised land with their own eyes. The people of that generation would die in the wilderness.

Through the judgment on the Israelites, we see the plan for how God will handle our unbelief. Just as the generation of doubters was killed off in the desert, every piece of our heart that doubts God must be killed through the process of sanctification. Everything within us that does not trust God fully must be put to death and pruned away. With Israel, God was finishing what He began by preserving His people as a nation, and with us God is finishing the work He began by perfecting and preparing us for the abundant life of tested faith.

He who called is faithful, and He will do it. The law of God is good. It drives us to realize our need for a Savior, and our Savior will make our faith complete and lacking in nothing.

Conclusion

God is raising His family, and He is doing so in love. His children need His law in order to understand some things about themselves and about God. The law serves as a tutor to reveal to them what they are desperately lacking—holiness.

God gave His family "the rules." Without the law, they could not distinguish holiness. They could not see their inability to be holy as God is holy. Without the law, they would not see their desperate need for Someone to step in and achieve holiness on their behalf. The law is the tutor that points to the need for a Savior.

The God who called us is faithful, and He will accomplish His purposes in our lives. The law of God is good. It shines a spotlight on the gracious and just character of God while pointing ahead to the Savior who will make our faith complete.

Prayer of *Response*

"Thou hast struck a heavy blow at my pride, at the false god of self, and I lie in pieces before thee. But thou hast given me another master and lord, thy Son, Jesus, and now my heart is turned towards holiness, my life speeds as an arrow from a bow towards complete obedience to thee. Help me in all my doings to put down sin and to humble pride. Save me from the love of the world and the pride of life, from everything that is natural to fallen man, and let Christ's nature be seen in me day by day. Grant me grace to bear thy will without repining, and delight to be not only chiselled, squared, or fashioned, but separated from the old rock where I have been embedded so long, and lifted from the quarry to the upper air, where I may be built in Christ for ever." [3]

–Puritan prayer

Devotions

A RIGHT PERSPECTIVE

The law gets a bad rap in our minds, doesn't it? When we think of the law, we often think of hundreds and hundreds of rules that are trying to crush us and make us slaves. Some of us have an even grimmer view of the law; the only words that come to mind when you think of the law are failure and defeat.

What if we have it all wrong? What if the law were a gracious gift to us, just like the other things God bestows upon us?

Let's look at the way David describes the law in the Psalms:

"The instruction of the LORD is perfect, renewing one's life; the testimony of the LORD is trustworthy, making the inexperienced wise. The precepts of the LORD are right, making the heart glad; the command of the LORD is radiant, making the eyes light up" (Ps. 19:7-8).

The law is meant to revive the soul. It is supposed to make the simple wise. It is given for the heart to rejoice. It is hard to have that perspective when we are constantly trying to attain our own salvation through the law; that is when the law becomes a chokehold. But this view is a distortion. We see rightly when we see that the law is a gracious gift that shines light on God's holiness and points forward to the gospel.

Pause and Reflect

1   What thoughts come to mind when you think of "the law"?

- -

2   Do you believe the law is meant for the good of the believer? Why do you think most people don't feel that way about it?

- -

3   Ask God to help your life and heart reflect what is true about His law.

FULFILLING THE LAW

It is sometimes difficult to define the relationship between the old and new covenants. Some people think about the covenants in the way they think about buying a new car. The old car becomes antiquated. It doesn't matter anymore because it has been substituted with a new car. Once the new car arrives, the old car is moot.

But we are wrong to think of the old covenant and God's law in this way. Jesus said:

"Don't assume that I came to destroy the Law or the Prophets. I did not come to destroy but to fulfill. For I assure you: Until heaven and earth pass away, not the smallest letter or one stroke of a letter will pass from the law until all things are accomplished" (Matt. 5:17-18).

You see, we are wrong to think that all the decrees within the law are irrelevant now that we have Jesus. The reality is that Jesus does not negate the law; instead, He fulfilled every single command with His obedience. All of the things that were demanded of us, Christ accomplished. The law mattered. It wasn't arbitrary.

The reality is that now, because of Jesus, we have a new law—the law of love. There is freedom in the commandments of Scripture. They are designed to bring about our best and our joy. Jesus did not only fulfill the law on our behalf, He also sent a Helper to us so that we too may be able to obey as He did in faith.

Jesus fulfilled the law so that we might find freedom in obedience.

Pause and Reflect

1   Is it hard for you to value the law in the Old Testament? If so, what are the obstacles?

- -

2   How does it make you feel that God would fulfill the standard of holiness on your behalf?

- -

3   How does the reality that God fulfilled every letter of the law affect the way you respond after success in your faith? What about in failure?

Lesson from the Israelites

The story of Israel failing to believe God is a story written down for us. God intends that we see ourselves in this story and be warned by Israel's example. We aren't better than the children of Israel. Our hearts are conditioned to doubt God and to fall away from the hope we have in Him—despite the many great wonders He has demonstrated through our lives.

The enemy of faith is unbelief. It causes us to reject the law and the commands of God as burdensome and tyrannical. God knows this about us and places in Scripture a warning for us—for me and you—about the importance of obeying His commands and believing that He is right.

Hebrews 3:7-13: "Therefore, as the Holy Spirit says: Today, if you hear His voice, do not harden your hearts as in the rebellion, on the day of testing in the wilderness, where your fathers tested Me, tried Me, and saw My works for 40 years. Therefore I was provoked with that generation and said, 'They always go astray in their hearts, and they have not known My ways.' So I swore in My anger, 'They will not enter My rest.' Watch out, brothers, so that there won't be in any of you an evil, unbelieving heart that departs from the living God. But encourage each other daily, while it is still called today, so that none of you is hardened by sin's deception."

We must fight for one another and challenge one another to believe the truth about God. Otherwise, sin will deceive us, like Israel, into thinking that God is against us rather than for us in Jesus Christ.

Pause and Reflect

1   Do you see yourself in Israel? How are you similar to them?

2   What importance do you see Hebrews 3:7-13 give to belief and encouragement?

3   How does your community of faith encourage you to believe the commands of God are good?

DISCUSSION QUESTIONS

1   What image comes to mind when you think of God's law? Could there be something really good and life-giving about God's law that we're missing?

2   Why is it that we often want to choose one attribute of God over the others? What would the world and your life be like if He were only gracious but not just? Or only just but not gracious? Why do we need Him to be both?

3   For some it's difficult to believe in a God who loves us in spite of our sin. For others it's difficult to believe in a God who will punish us because we are guilty. Why is it important to discern people's view of God as we share the gospel with them?

4   In what ways do our modern-day "gods" (idols) demand sacrifices of our time and money? Why do people sacrifice health, family, and time for these gods?

5   In what ways is the commandment in Deuteronomy 6:4-5 both simple and profound? What does it look like for us to love God with the different dimensions of our being (heart, soul, and strength)? Why should our goal be to love God with everything?

6   The law reflects God's character, and God's reaction to Israel's sin and Moses' pleading gives us a glimpse of His holiness and mercy. In what ways should our hearts mirror Moses' as we plead for people who do not know Christ?

7   How is our mission to others affected by aligning our heart with God's heart for the world? Why is it true that those who love God will overflow with love for others?

8   God's action toward the unbelieving Israelites was severe. How does God's severe response to unbelief help us see the importance of trusting God as we seek to walk in His ways? How does God's promise to perfect the work He has begun in us give us confidence to persevere in obedience during trials and temptations?

9   Why is it important that we understand how grace preceded the giving of God's law? What is the danger of thinking grace is what we earn with our law-keeping?

Part 2

GOD DEVELOPS HIS COVENANT PEOPLE

God's covenant with Abraham began God's people Israel. Despite the people's sin and idolatry, God remained faithful to His covenant. He brought them out of slavery in Egypt and placed them in the promised land. He raised up a king after His own heart to shepherd His people. He gave them His presence and peace, songs to sing, and wisdom to live by. Yet these blessings all point to something greater.

Chapter 6

The Land

God's Place for His Covenant People

VOICES FROM *the Church*

"The heroes of the faith had one thing in common: They were all ordinary people with no power of their own. The difference is the mighty presence of God."[1]
   –Henry Blackaby

VOICES FROM *Church History*

"Let your spirit be joyful in God your Saviour, the joy of the Lord shall be your strength, and no fiend of hell shall make headway against you."[2]
   –Charles Spurgeon (1834-1892)

Search for "lottery winners years later" on the Internet and you'll find a long list of tragic stories. A New Jersey woman won $5.4 million in the 1980s. A gambler, the money is now gone and she lives in a trailer. A West Virginia businessman won the lottery, set up a charity, but was later arrested for drunk driving and threatening a bar manager. A 19-year-old British garbage man won the lottery. He bought a luxurious home and a fleet of cars. By the age of 26, after years of wild partying, he was living on a government unemployment check.

In these examples, a person was given a gift that promised to satisfy physical needs and to provide rest from hard labor. But they quickly proved unable to wisely steward that gift. The problem was not incompetence; it was their appetite, their wrongful desire, their idolatry. Each sought their ultimate joy and salvation in satisfying an insatiable appetite. Like a car chase in a movie, their mad pursuit for satisfying their sinful appetites caused them to run over everything that stood in their way.

As Christians, we know that apart from God's grace, we would squander great treasure because that is what our father Adam did in the garden of Eden. Indeed, this is one of the main lessons of the entire Old Testament: Human beings—even when they have all the advantages of God's words, provision, and presence—forsake God and choose other gods.

This chapter covers the books of Joshua, Judges, and Ruth. In these books we see the people of Israel turn away from God and experience His discipline. It's almost as if God means for these history books to say to us, "Did you miss the point of Adam and Eve? Then let Me build a bigger stage and repeat the story." Sure enough, whole nations rise and fall. Peoples and leaders come and go. One lesson becomes very clear: All people sin and fall short of God's righteousness and glory. We need something more than the resources inside of us. We need something from the outside—God's grace.

A generous and faithful God gives His people a land (Josh. 1:1-9).

In the Bible's story line, the people of Israel were standing on the edge of the promised land. They had been wandering in the wilderness for 40 years after the exodus from Egypt. Moses gave them three sermons (the Book of Deuteronomy). Then he died. Now God tells Moses' assistant, the nation's new leader, Joshua, to lead them into the land.

As you read the passage, take a close look at what God promised His people in the past that He is here delivering (vv. 1-4). Also look at the new promises He made (vv. 5-9).

1 *After the death of Moses the* LORD's *servant, the* LORD *spoke to Joshua son of Nun, who had served Moses:* 2 *"Moses My servant is dead. Now you and all the people prepare to cross over the Jordan to the land I am giving the Israelites.* 3 *I have given you every place where the sole of your foot treads, just as I promised Moses.* 4 *Your territory will be from the wilderness and Lebanon to the great Euphrates River—all the land of the Hittites—and west to the Mediterranean Sea.* 5 *No one will be able to stand against you as long as you live. I will be with you, just as I was with Moses. I will not leave you or forsake you.*

6 *"Be strong and courageous, for you will distribute the land I swore to their fathers to give them as an inheritance.* 7 *Above all, be strong and very courageous to carefully observe the whole instruction My servant Moses commanded you. Do not turn from it to the right or the left, so that you will have success wherever you go.* 8 *This book of instruction must not depart from your mouth; you are to recite it day and night so that you may carefully observe everything written in it. For then you will prosper and succeed in whatever you do.* 9 *Haven't I commanded you: be strong and courageous? Do not be afraid or discouraged, for the* LORD *your God is with you wherever you go."*

This land was a gift from God. He promised in the past to give them a land. And notice He marked off its dimensions. God does not deliver on His promises vaguely; He delivers concretely. Get out a tape measure and measure it! Look down and see the dirt stuck in the treads of your boots, and consider the fact that God keeps His promises.

Here He promises three things: Their enemies will not defeat them. He will be with them. He will not forsake them. And the people were to trust these promises because He had proven that He keeps His word.

God promises to keep those who are His. He promises not to forsake us. He promises not to let anything come between us and His love. He promises that His yoke is easy and His burden is light. He promises to conform us to the image of His Son. He promises not to let us fall into a temptation for which He will not also provide a way of escape. He promises to occasionally discipline us as a son whom He loves. He promises that a day is coming when He will come to claim His people and that all strife and tears will cease and that we will be with Him forever.

The problem is not that God has not made promises to us or that He doesn't keep those promises. It's that either we don't believe what He says or we're not interested in what He promises because we still love the world too much.

In the remainder of the passage, God tells Joshua how he, and the people, should respond to the gift of the land. In verses 6-7, God commands Joshua to be strong and courageous *to carefully observe* the instruction—the law—He had given to Moses. He expands on this second command in verse 8 by telling Joshua to keep His word in his mouth, to recite it day and night. What would be the result of keeping these two basic commands? God promised that they would prosper and succeed in whatever they did.

We're more accustomed to equating obedience and the fear of the Lord, as the Book of Proverbs talks about. But these verses give us the flip side: Obedience to God can be equated with a kind of strength and courage in the face of the world and its threats. That's precisely why Jesus said we should not fear those who kill the body but are not able to kill the soul; rather, we're to fear Him who is able to destroy both soul and body in hell (Matt. 10:28).

Don't be afraid of people who will make fun of you for being a Christian. Don't be afraid of those who might persecute you. Don't be afraid of losing your job, your family, or your life. Be strong and courageous. God alone is to be feared. Obey Him.

Often it's our fear of the world that lies behind our disobedience. We fear what we might lose: our reputation, our money, our job, our safety, our lusts, our ambitions, even our life. So we try to take control of our circumstances and do whatever it takes to hold on to what we want.

Knowing that God is generous and faithful to His promises helps us be strong and courageous because we can trust His character as we pour out our lives for Him.

This means that as Christians, we can be generous with our money and time, knowing that God cares for us and will provide for us. Don't worry!

This means we can take the gospel to tough neighborhoods and hostile nations, knowing that God will keep His promises—that His sheep in those neighborhoods and nations *will hear* His voice and that nothing can separate us from His love. Don't fear!

This means that we can have the courage to be faithful as parents and as spouses, doing what is right in those relationships day after day, even though the results are not always visible. Don't be anxious!

A rebellious people reject God's rule (Judg. 2:11-19).

Sadly, the people of Israel were not strong and courageous to obey. Instead, they rejected God's rule, which brings us to the Book of Judges, where God's rebellious people reject His rule. Judges 2:11-19 provides us with a sample and a summary of the book:

11 *The Israelites did what was evil in the* LORD'*s sight. They worshiped the Baals* 12 *and abandoned the* LORD, *the God of their fathers, who had brought them out of Egypt. They went after other gods from the surrounding peoples and bowed down to them. They infuriated the* LORD, 13 *for they abandoned Him and worshiped Baal and the Ashtoreths.*

14 *The* LORD'*s anger burned against Israel, and He handed them over to marauders who raided them. He sold them to the enemies around them, and they could no longer resist their enemies.* 15 *Whenever the Israelites went out, the* LORD *was against them and brought disaster on them, just as He had promised and sworn to them. So they suffered greatly.*

16 *The* LORD *raised up judges, who saved them from the power of their marauders,* 17 *but they did not listen to their judges. Instead, they prostituted themselves with other gods, bowing down to them. They quickly turned from the way of their fathers, who had walked in obedience to the* LORD'*s commands. They did not do as their fathers did.* 18 *Whenever the* LORD *raised up a judge for the Israelites, the* LORD *was with him and saved the people from the power of their enemies while the judge was still alive. The* LORD *was moved to pity whenever they groaned because of those who were oppressing and afflicting them.* 19 *Whenever the judge died, the Israelites would act even more corruptly than their fathers, going after other gods to worship and bow down to them. They did not turn from their evil practices or their obstinate ways.*

Remember how I said that God uses the history of the Old Testament to make the point clear that all people sin and need something from outside of themselves to rescue them from their sin? The Book of Judges is like a corkscrew that pushes this lesson deeper and deeper with each twist of the narrative cycle: "Whenever the judge died, the Israelites would act even more corruptly than their fathers."

God blessed His people beyond what any lottery winner might dream of. He gave them a land flowing with milk and honey. He promised peace on all their borders. He gave them just laws, including provisions even for the poor. Most of all, He gave them His own presence. He said they would be a kingdom of priests, a chosen nation, and His treasured possession. The Israelites had hit the jackpot, not by chance but by God's own loving choice.

But like the lottery winners, God's people squandered His gifts. Verse 17 uses the language of "prostituting themselves" with other gods. To prostitute yourself means to take something that is most precious and wrongly exchange it for cash, thereby disobeying God as well as trashing that which is precious. And that's what the people did.

Throughout Scripture God uses the analogy of marriage to teach us about the relationship He means to have with His people. It's to be a relationship that's holy, chaste, jealous, exclusive, tender, affectionate, passionate, and intimate. It's to be a relationship that changes our very identity. You see this in how God talks about Israel. They are *His people*, and He is *their God*. And you see this in how God talks about the church. Husbands are told to love their wives by looking to the example of how Christ loves the church.

By the same token, Scripture uses the pictures of prostitution and adultery to teach us what's happening whenever we sin and disobey. We are taking something precious (our lives, our worship) and giving it to someone who only exploits and uses us (the world, the flesh, and the Devil), and we are doing it for a few measly dollar bills that will be gone before the day is done. How tragic sin is! How wretched and sad! We could enjoy the delights of faithful marital intimacy and fellowship, but instead, we choose the exploitation, degradation, and diseases of one-night stands. Every time we sin, that's what we're doing.

As non-Christians, we resisted God's grace again and again. He gave us good gift after good gift, but we continued to spurn Him for the sake of self-rule and selfish gain. And sadly, even as Christians, we continue to do the very things we don't want to do and leave undone the things we should do (see Rom. 7).

The point here is not to wallow and grovel in our badness; it's to recognize honestly what we are and then direct our eyes outside of ourselves to a Savior. And that brings us to the judges themselves.

The judges were the men and women appointed by God to rescue God's sinful people from their enemies and to judge the people's disputes. You might have heard their names—Gideon, Barak, Deborah, Samson, Jephthah, and so on. The Book of Hebrews tells us they lived by faith for the purpose of enforcing justice and obtaining the promises of God (Heb. 11:32-34).

The larger lesson to take from the figures of the judges is that they were God's appointed, Spirit-empowered rescuers of God's sinful people. What's their purpose? Take Samson, for instance. The point is not "Be a masculine man like Samson" but rather "God's people need a powerful conqueror who can smash the enemies of God and His people, the very enemies leading the sinful people astray."

And that brings us to the Book of Ruth and our third main lesson.

A gracious God promises to restore His people from the nations (Ruth 4:14-17).

The Book of Ruth is like a little gem set in the midst of the dark days recounted in the Book of Judges. It tells the story of a man who leaves famine-ridden Israel with his wife and two sons in search of food and work but then promptly dies. His sons die as well, but only after marrying foreign women. By verse 5 of the book, you find yourself standing in a foreign land with three mourning widows, one of whom was fleeing starvation—not an auspicious beginning. Naomi, the mother-in-law of the other two, wanted to be called "Mara," which means bitter. The Lord had dealt bitterly with her, she said.

Eventually, the famine in Israel ends, and one of the daughters-in-law, Ruth, agrees to return with Naomi in order to share her burdens and struggles. Back in Israel, this foreign daughter-in-law goes to work in the field of a man named Boaz, who demonstrates abundant kindness to both Ruth and Naomi. Ruth and Boaz end up marrying; Ruth bears a son; and that son, we learn in the book's final verses, turns out to be the grandfather of King David.

14 *Then the women said to Naomi, "Praise the LORD, who has not left you without a family redeemer today. May his name become well known in Israel.* 15 *He will renew your life and sustain you in your old age. Indeed, your daughter-in-law, who loves you and is better to you than seven sons, has given birth to him." * 16 *Naomi took the child, placed him on her lap, and took care of him.* 17 *The neighbor women said, "A son has been born to Naomi," and they named him Obed. He was the father of Jesse, the father of David.*

There are lots of good moral lessons we can take from the characters of the story. From Ruth we learn to share the burdens of others. From Boaz we learn to care for our neighbors, even neighbors who might seem strange because they come from another place.

But God is first and at the center of this love story. "Praise the LORD!" said the women. God brought the widows back. God ended the famine and grew the barley for harvest. God instructed the people of Israel to make provisions for the poor. God showed mercy to Israelite and foreigner alike. God enabled Ruth to conceive (4:13). And God brought Boaz, the family redeemer (v. 14). The Book of Ruth is sweet because it should cause us to praise God!

Second, the emphasis falls on Boaz, the family redeemer who graciously gives of himself for the needy and heavy-laden. He makes provision for a woman who would name herself "Bitter." And like the judges, he points us to another Redeemer who would come to give life and hope to a needy people.

The book ends with King David—the man after God's own heart who pictured the righteous rule of God in the New Testament. He was the king to whom the promises to Adam and then Abraham were pointing. More importantly, Jesus taught us that David pointed to the One who was greater than David—Jesus Himself. He is the true seed to whom all the promises of God point, which is why it is not surprising that Ruth ends with a genealogy.

These last words in the Book of Ruth, which pile together the image of a family redeemer and the image of King David, are meant to give us a whiff, you might say, of Jesus. The Book of Ruth ultimately points us to Jesus, our Redeemer and our King! And Jesus sent His disciples to all nations, including our own cities, to proclaim His redeeming and kingly work.

Conclusion

As Christians, we can rejoice because God has not left us alone in our sins but has given us evangelists who taught us the Word of the gospel. He has not left us without instructions for how to live but has given His Bible and pastors to teach us the Bible. He has not left us to carry our personal burdens alone or to rejoice alone, but He has given us a church body to share our burdens and joys. He has not abandoned us to unrighteous and trashed-out lives, but He is sanctifying us together to be a holy and loving people. He has placed His name upon us (we are Christ-ians). He has said that we are His treasured possession. And He promises to restore us fully to Himself, no matter what the world throws at us in the meantime.

God has given us a Judge, Redeemer, and King who is Christ, and then He has given us one another for continually pointing one another to Him. And just like the Christlike Boaz, we should continually look for ways to bless those who stand in need of our care. By doing so, we point them to Christ!

What do the Old Testament histories teach us? They teach us that amidst our sin, we can find hope and comfort in the fact that God is generous to give. God is faithful to keep His promises. God is just to judge. God is merciful and glorious to restore. And God has a purpose for the nations.

Devotions

REST

Hebrews 4:8-9: "For if Joshua had given them rest, God would not have spoken later about another day. Therefore, a Sabbath rest remains for God's people."

Ah, finally the promised land. They'd arrived. They could sit down, kick off their sandals, and put up their feet. Rest. How they needed it! After slave drivers in Egypt and scorpion stings in the wilderness, Joshua ushered the people of Israel into a land flowing with milk and honey. God had promised they would find safe harbor here from all their enemies. Bread baskets were supposed to bulge, as were the wombs of their merry young wives. All good gifts, no doubt.

But you know what? This wasn't the end. The promised land wasn't their ultimate rest. It was just a shadow that pointed to something greater, like the paper-thin slice of shade attached at the heels of a real-live person standing in sunshine.

Imagine stepping from a 2-D world into a 3-D world—how gripping, pulsating, and delicious life would suddenly become. That's the difference between the rest the best things of this world offer and the rest of dwelling in the presence of Christ forever.

Where does your heart look for its rest? If only it were the weekend…if only I were married…if only I got that promotion…if only I could get control of my schedule…if only I could get out of this town…if only I could get that house. Do you really want to spend your life striving after two-dimensional shadows?

Take stock of all of God's good gifts to you and thank Him. But then strive to enter His rest and don't become disobedient (4:11). God is saying to you, "You think these things are good? Just you wait—I'm even better!"

Pause and Reflect

1   What are some of God's best earthly gifts to you?

- -

2   How are you tempted to find wrongful rest, peace, and joy in them?

- -

3   How can you enjoy them rightly? How can you let them point you to Him?

Abandoning the Lord

Judges 10:6: "Then the Israelites again did what was evil in the sight of the LORD. They worshiped the Baals and the Ashtoreths, the gods of Aram, Sidon, and Moab, and the gods of the Ammonites and the Philistines. They abandoned Yahweh and did not worship Him."

Had not the Lord done great things for the nation of Israel? He had rescued them from Egypt and given them a land flowing with milk and honey. But in the Book of Judges, we encounter this astonishing line: "They abandoned Yahweh."

Abandoned. Israel was like a wife who abandons her faithful and affectionate husband. Or like a child who abandons good and loving parents. Why? They wanted to worship the gods of the surrounding peoples. No, these gods had not made promises and kept them. These were idols made of wood who couldn't speak! But something about them was enticing. Maybe it was social approval. Maybe it was the talk of earthly gain. Maybe these gods seemed new and exciting, not like grandpa's old religion.

This much we can assume: worshiping the gods of the nations always makes sense in the moment. We don't worship what seems ludicrous. We worship what sounds rational and wise by the standards of the day. When the heart wants something, it finds a reason to justify it. Then, slowly and imperceptibly, the heart begins to darken, thinking becomes futile, and you abandon the God who loves you (see Rom. 1:21).

Don't take for granted what everyone around you takes for granted— look to God's Word. Be watchful over your heart's deepest longings as well as its rationalizations. Then pray you would not abandon your first love, Jesus Christ (Rev. 2:4).

Pause and Reflect

1   What are some common idols of your country or ethnic group that you might take for granted? What rationalizations might you give?

- -

2   How can you fight these enticements with the gospel?

Empty for Filling

Ruth 1:20-22: "'Don't call me Naomi. Call me Mara,' she answered, 'for the Almighty has made me very bitter. I went away full, but the LORD has brought me back empty. Why do you call me Naomi, since the LORD has pronounced judgment on me, and the Almighty has afflicted me?' So Naomi came back from the land of Moab with her daughter-in-law Ruth the Moabitess. They arrived in Bethlehem at the beginning of the barley harvest."

There's Naomi walking back to Judah. She left with a husband and two sons, now they are dead. You understand her bitterness, right? The Lord has brought her back empty, she says—sort of true. He has certainly emptied her of what she once had.

Yet move your eyes from Naomi to the other one. Isn't that Ruth, whom God sent to Judah to provide for Naomi? Won't Ruth bear a son who will ensure Naomi's prosperity and usher in an even greater promise for the nation—a mighty king?

Now look at the scenery around them. What's there? Rolling fields of golden barley. She had left in famine, but she returns in plenty. The barley harvest has begun.

The Lord does empty us, but He empties us so He can fill us. What's more, He is working even in our emptiest moments, when hope has fled. Quietly He puts the pieces in place, preparing us for the plenty ahead. Our hearts want to find peace in the things of this world, but kindly and patiently He teaches us that peace can only be found in Him.

Do not waste time in foolish bitterness when trials come. Trust instead, Christian, that your loving Father is working out His redemption in your life—perfectly.

Pause and Reflect

1   What is your first reaction when trials hit?

- -

2   Read Romans 8:28. What comfort does this verse and Naomi's experience give to Christians in the midst of trials?

DISCUSSION QUESTIONS

1   Why are most of us tempted to think, *I would have done better*? How does the Bible challenge the idea that we would do better?

- -

2   What are some promises that God has made to us today? Do we live according to these promises? Why or why not?

- -

3   What are some things God has NOT promised to His people but Christians sometimes demand from Him anyway?

- -

4   What is the link between courage and obedience to God's Word? What can we then assume is behind so much disobedience to God's Word?

- -

5   How does assurance of God's generosity and faithfulness lead us to be strong and courageous?

- -

6   Thinking of lottery winners, in what sense might we say the people of Israel hit the jackpot? In what ways does Israel resemble lottery winners who utterly squandered the gift they had been given?

- -

7   What are some of the good gifts of God that people squander? How does our sin cheapen God's good gifts (creation, sex, family, etc.)?

- -

8   In what ways do we reflect the rebellious people of Israel—both before and after coming to Christ?

- -

9   If you had to guess by the book's name, who often receives the most attention when this book is talked about? Now look at verse 14. Where does its emphasis fall?

Chapter 7

The Kings

God Raises Up Kings to Lead His People

In the classic movie *Mr. Smith Goes to Washington,* Jimmy Stewart plays the role of the young, idealistic Jefferson Smith who is appointed a U.S. Senator. When Senator Smith first arrives in Washington, he dreamily boards a sight-seeing bus headed for the capital city's sites. At the Supreme Court Building, he looks up at the sacred words inscribed in marble: "Equal Justice." Then in a moment intended to evoke a sense of majesty, he slowly ascends the stairs of the Lincoln Memorial to gaze upon the massive statue of this greatest of presidents. Alas, if only this world's leaders were as majestic as their monuments! A few short scenes later, Senator Smith finds himself face down in the muck of DC corruption and power politics.

Since the history of the world, not one nation has been without corruption. Not one has lived up to the ideals it has inscribed on its monuments. And it's on this landscape of fallen nations and futile kings that the story of Israel and its rulers is set.

As the period of the "judges" came to an end, God was Israel's only king. But the people called for "a king to judge us the same as all the other nations have" (1 Sam. 8:5). At first, God gave them the kind of king they were looking for. King Saul was tall and handsome. But he was impetuous and foolish, jealous and paranoid. He even massacred an entire city—men, women, and children (22:11-19). "Build your pretty monuments if you want," God seemed to say, "but do you really want to put your hope here?"

But God did something unexpected. The people might have wanted a king for bad reasons, but God used for good what they meant for evil. God *will* rule His people through a human king, and He *will* make His glory known through such a king.

The message for Jefferson Smith and for us is this: You're right to place all your hopes in a great Leader, to believe that His government will bring equal justice for all as well as life, liberty, and happiness. But you're not going to find these in the governments or nations of this world. You're going to find them in an unlikely place and in an unlikely Leader.

In this chapter we see God's commitment to lead the people of Israel by raising up kings who represent the people to God and God to the people. Ultimately, Israel's longing (and our own) for the world to be ruled rightly points to the Messiah—promised to King David and awaited by God's people. Meanwhile, God's people make His name known to the world through their obedience to His commands.

God will rule His people through a human king (2 Sam. 7:11b-16).

After the ruinous reign of King Saul, God enthroned a man after His own heart—David. God had secured his kingdom. God had given him victory over his enemies, such as the Philistines. When David expressed to God his desire to build a temple, God surprised him with a list of extravagant promises:

11b *"The LORD declares to you: The LORD Himself will make a house for you. 12 When your time comes and you rest with your fathers, I will raise up after you your descendant, who will come from your body, and I will establish his kingdom. 13 He will build a house for My name, and I will establish the throne of his kingdom forever. 14 I will be a father to him, and he will be a son to Me. When he does wrong, I will discipline him with a human rod and with blows from others. 15 But My faithful love will never leave him as I removed it from Saul; I removed him from your way. 16 Your house and kingdom will endure before Me forever, and your throne will be established forever.'"*

God is King, and yet from this passage we see that His plan is to rule His people *through* a human being. Just a few verses before God made these promises, He told David: "I took you from the pasture and from following the sheep to be ruler over My people Israel" (v. 8). The people were not David's people, they were God's people. But God made David the ruler over them. God decided to rule His people through this human king. He would use a mediator. Why? God, whom we cannot see, intended to use a human king to teach the world what He is like.

Notice also the focus on David's son: "I will be a father to him, and he will be a son to Me." Why the image of a father-son relationship? In the Hebrew mind, sons look like their father, act like their father, and follow in their father's professional footsteps. To use the language of Genesis 1, sons bear their father's image. David's royal son was to bear the image of God so that when people looked at him and his rule, they would think of God.

So grandiose were these promises to David that we begin to see that God was pointing to another, greater King. At first it's clear that God was speaking about David's son Solomon. Yes, Solomon did build a house for God. But it's hard to miss the allusion to something even greater than Solomon: "I will establish the throne of his kingdom forever" (v. 13). Forever? Really? That's a long time.

God did fulfill these promises to David and his son Solomon. But He fulfilled them completely in Jesus Christ, the greater Son of David. Ultimately, God will rule His people through a human King, whose name is Jesus.

Go back to Jefferson Smith for a moment, standing there at the Lincoln Memorial, hat removed and face filled with awe. It's true we should give thanks for just and godly leaders. At the same time, we must never forget that first and foremost, Christians are citizens of heaven. Praise God for leaders and nations that seek equal justice and life, liberty, and happiness. But we must remember that ultimately these things will be found in the gospel of Jesus Christ. In their absolutely best moments, the governments of this world can only provide a shadow of what our Savior and King—Jesus—will provide.

So how does this truth affect our view of earthly leaders? First, we obey human governments, knowing that they have been instituted and authorized by King Jesus. They are His servant and agent (Rom. 13:1-7). We should also pray for them. But we should never disobey Jesus, even if other authorities in this world call us to do so.

Second, we should never let our national identity and national values define us more than our Christian identity and Christian values. Our churches should not be gatherings of Americans; they should be gatherings of Christians who may or may not be American. What can you do to make internationals feel welcome?

Third, we should strive with whatever opportunities the Lord gives us in government—voting, policing, soldiering, adjudicating, legislating—to love Christ and to love our neighbors. Christians should work hard for peace, justice, prosperity, and the safety of our neighbors because we love them. And we should do this so that through our lives and fruit, our non-Christian neighbors get a more accurate picture of Christ and His rule. All of us have been given rule over something, even if it's just a voting ballot or a Boy Scout troop. And we want to use whatever rule we have to produce good in the lives of others, just as Jesus does through His rule.

Finally, even as we work hard for good government, we do so with a loose grip, knowing that our true Savior and King is Jesus, not our favorite presidential or congressional candidate. Jesus is the hope of the nations.

God will rule an unlikely people through an unlikely king (2 Sam. 7:18-24).

18 *Then King David went in, sat in the LORD's presence, and said,*
Who am I, Lord GOD, and what is my house that You have brought me this
far? 19 *What You have done so far was a little thing to You, Lord GOD, for You*
have also spoken about Your servant's house in the distant future. And this is
a revelation for mankind, Lord GOD. 20 *What more can David say to You?*
You know Your servant, Lord GOD. 21 *Because of Your word and according to*
Your will, You have revealed all these great things to Your servant.

22 This is why You are great, Lord GOD. There is no one like You, and there is no God besides You, as all we have heard confirms. 23 And who is like Your people Israel? God came to one nation on earth in order to redeem a people for Himself, to make a name for Himself, and to perform for them great and awesome acts, driving out nations and their gods before Your people You redeemed for Yourself from Egypt. 24 You established Your people Israel to be Your own people forever, and You, LORD, have become their God.

Notice the first words out of David's mouth in response to all these great promises: "Who am I?! Who am I that You've done as much as You already have and that You promise to do more? I'm a seventh son. I was just a shepherd. I sin like everyone else. Who am I?" David saw himself as an unlikely king and mediator for God, but he trusted in God's greatness: "I'm not God. You are!"

It's this contrast between the greatness of God and the unlikely nature of servants that runs through this whole section. Notice that David also mentioned the uniqueness of the people of Israel, yet he did so not to highlight their greatness but God's (v. 23). The people of God are unique not because of any quality of their own—their righteousness, their greatness—but because *God* redeemed them. He was making a name for Himself through them.

The children of Israel were an unlikely people with an unlikely king. And all this unlikeliness points forward to Jesus—and to us. The prophet Isaiah spoke of the ordinariness of the Messiah (Isa. 53:2). The apostle Paul reminded the Corinthian church of their plainness as well (1 Cor. 1:26-29). Every Christian should have the humble attitude of King David: "Who am I that God would save me? I'm not wise. I'm not of noble birth. Who am I?" If David had no reason to boast, how much less should *you* and *I* boast!

When we fail to grasp the marvelous grace of the gospel, we struggle for pride and control. We have too high a view of ourselves and too low a view of God. Instead of saying, "Who am I?" we give ourselves credit for what we are—either in the world or as Christians. We forget the Son of God had to become a human and die on the cross to pay the penalty for our sins in order to redeem us to God.

One of the best ways to grow in humility is to grow in your knowledge of who God is and what He has done. He is the beginning and the end, the Creator and Sustainer of all things. God is weaving together all of our story lines from beginning to end, from the president to the homeless man on the street to you. And on the last day, we will all behold the mini-narratives of our lives together with the grand narrative of history, and we will worship. We will say, "Yes, You are good, and You are just. You are God, and there is no other."

Do you long for justice in this world? Look to God in Christ, who is the source of all justice. Do you need wisdom? Christ alone is our wisdom, and He gives wisdom generously to whoever asks. Are you looking for love? God is love. He is the source of love, the grounds of love, the energy of love, the life of love, and the hope of love.

Our entire lives are circumscribed by the curves of His hands because we are in them. He gives you your breath. He plans your days. He is your Judge. There is no one like Him, and there is no God besides Him. The only question is "Are we His enemy or friend?"

God will make His name known through the obedience of His people (1 Kings 8:54-61).

God kept His promise to David. He gave the kingdom to David's son Solomon, and then Solomon built a house for God—the temple. God had chosen an unlikely king and an unlikely people with whom to dwell. God's personal presence was most evident in the temple. They could see His presence in the form of a cloud, just as the people wandering through the wilderness could see Him leading them in the pillar of cloud.

At the temple's dedication, Solomon prayed, acknowledging that "even heaven, the highest heaven, cannot contain You, much less this temple I have built" (8:27). Here is the ending of His prayer:

54 *When Solomon finished praying this entire prayer and petition to the* Lord, *he got up from kneeling before the altar of the* Lord, *with his hands spread out toward heaven,* 55 *and he stood and blessed the whole congregation of Israel with a loud voice:* 56 *"May the* Lord *be praised! He has given rest to His people Israel according to all He has said. Not one of all the good promises He made through His servant Moses has failed.* 57 *May the* Lord *our God be with us as He was with our ancestors. May He not abandon us or leave us* 58 *so that He causes us to be devoted to Him, to walk in all His ways, and to keep His commands, statutes, and ordinances, which He commanded our ancestors.* 59 *May my words I have made my petition with before the* Lord *be near the* Lord *our God day and night, so that He may uphold His servant's cause and the cause of His people Israel, as each day requires,* 60 *and so that all the peoples of the earth may know that Yahweh is God. There is no other!* 61 *Let your heart be completely devoted to the* Lord *our God to walk in His statutes and to keep His commands, as it is today."*

Let's look at what Solomon asked of God. In the first invocation, Solomon praises God. In the second and third, he announces his desire for God to be with the people and not to abandon them. Then in the fourth, he observes that it must be God who helps them obey His commands. God must incline their hearts—"You tell me to obey, God, but now give the obedience You command." Then the reasons for the first four invocations are explained in the fifth: "Stay with us and help us obey so that everyone on earth will know that there is no God but You." The call to obedience is then reaffirmed in the final invitation (v. 61).

After beginning with praise, Solomon asked God to be with the people and not to abandon them. Then he recognized that God would be the One to help them obey His commands. God would need to incline their hearts toward obedience. The ultimate reason for the people's obedience was so "all the peoples of the earth may know that Yahweh is God. There is no other!" (v. 60).

The entire story of Israel, not to mention the story of our own lives, demonstrates that we cannot obey God apart from God's help. He must place His law "within" us, which He promises to do through the new covenant.

Think about it like this: Everything operates according to some set of laws. From computers to photocopy machines, from governments to giraffes, everything that moves is governed by some set of laws. The same is true for sinners and saints. A sinner, by nature, sins. Sin is the law that governs a sinner. What a sinner needs, therefore, is for God to place a new law within his or her heart—a new operating principle.

A Christian has been given this new nature. Through the Spirit, God has placed a new law within those who belong to Christ. But the old nature lives within us still. Therefore, we do battle to live by the law of the new nature and not the old. The good news of Christianity is that God has canceled the guilt of our sin so that we're no longer under God's judgment, and He has broken the power of sin so that we no longer must obey sin's desires. We are now free to obey by the power of God's Spirit. That's why we pray, along with Solomon: Cause our hearts to obey You, Lord!

Conclusion

Solomon asked God to help the people obey for the sake of God's name. The New Testament repeats this same lesson. Jesus said we're to let people see our good works so they give praise to the Father in heaven (Matt. 5:16). Peter said to do good deeds so the nations would glorify God (1 Pet. 2:12). Jesus also said that people will know we are His disciples by our love for one another as Christians (John 13:34-35).

As God's people living under the rule of Christ our King, our life together should serve as the backdrop for our evangelism. Church members should go out with the powerful words of the gospel, but our lives both *together* and *apart* should commend those words.

When the world sees Christians *together*, they should see us fighting for love and holiness:
• We're quick to forgive when offense is given.
• We repent of bitterness toward one another.
• We build our lives around each other, showing frequent hospitality.
• We gently correct one another in sin. We keep one another accountable.

When the world sees Christians *apart*, they should see us doing good for our neighbors:
• As employers, Christians should be known for giving fair wages and equal opportunities.
• As employees, Christians should be known for being hard working, honest, not gossips, peacemakers.
• As friends, Christians are the ones asking questions, taking interest in others.
• As citizens, Christians seek the good of neighbors as God gives opportunity.
• As extended family members, Christians are the ones to make sacrifices for the family's good. We're the ones willing to clean up afterward. We're the ones willing to speak the tough word when others are afraid or to keep our mouths shut when others spout folly.

So let's pray like Solomon: Oh God, may You cause our hearts to be devoted to You, to walk in all Your ways, and to keep Your commands, statutes, and ordinances so that You may uphold my cause as a Christian and our cause as a church and so that all the peoples of the earth may know that the Lord is God. There is no other!

Devotions

POWERFUL NAME

1 Samuel 17:45: "David said to the Philistine: 'You come against me with a dagger, spear, and sword, but I come against you in the name of Yahweh of Hosts, the God of Israel's armies—you have defied Him.'"

Picture in your head what Goliath's forearms must have looked like. They probably looked like something carved out of granite by a great sculptor or like one of those ropes that tie a mighty ocean liner to the pier. They must have been hard, sinewy, and massive. If you had arms like that, it would be easy to trust your dagger, spear, or sword, wouldn't it?

Humans have always wanted to trust their own strength, riches, beauty, or intelligence. Even when not impressive on the outside, we still rely on our wits, our gumption, our can-do spirit. David had killed a bear and a lion with his arms; however, he didn't trust his arms. He stood before Goliath holding a sling and five stones—true—but listen to this boast: "I come against you in the name of Yahweh of Hosts."

David knew the Lord would defend His own name. And he belonged to the people to whom the Lord had attached His name. You can almost see the party sticker on David's shirt: "Hello, I'm with GOD." He knew there was no safer place on earth, safer than the one who says, "I'm with the general," or, "I'm with the president."

Has Christ placed His name on you? Are you a Christ-ian? If so, be bold. At work, at home, in the nice parts and the not-so-nice parts of town, be courageous. Proclaim the name of the Lord Jesus. It's a dangerous enterprise, as dangerous as a battlefield. But the Lord will ultimately vindicate all those who bear His name. You're His, and His reputation is now staked on you. Do you think He'll let you go?

Pause and Reflect

1   Why is there great comfort and security in saying, "I'm with Jesus"?

----

2   What is one bold action you can take today knowing that you wear His name and that He will vindicate you?

Toward Eden

1 Kings 6:35: "He carved cherubim, palm trees, and flower blossoms on them and overlaid them with gold applied evenly over the carving."

The decor on the temple in Jerusalem was to be lush. Like paradise. Like the luxurious vegetation of Eden. That's what these golden palm trees and flower blossoms were supposed to remind people of. So were the golden cherubim. Remember how when God evicted Adam from Eden, He placed cherubim with flaming swords at the entrance to guard it? Jerusalem's temple was the place of the Lord, just as Eden was the place of the Lord. And the place of the Lord is a luxurious place, a resplendent place, a dangerous place.

Is a church's gathering to be a place of prosperity and peril, resplendence and risk? Yes! When the church gathers, it's not the cherubim's sword that swings but the sword of the Word. It divides people from their worldly loves and cuts believers in two, splitting the old from the new. Do you have a secret lust that you continue to coddle, a vain ambition that still has your eye? The fellowship of believers is where such things can be lovingly drawn into the light and then kindly killed.

When the church gathers, it's not lush vegetation that we smell but the aroma of Christ. Are you broken, hurting, sinful? Smell the love that believers share with one another. Behold the buds of forgiveness. Refresh yourself in streams of service. Perhaps your church is no Eden. That's true. But if it's a church where the gospel is believed, you are traveling together toward it, little by little. You're following the One who bared His neck to the cherub's sword so that you could enter. The tree of life awaits (see Rev. 22:2,14,19). It's just ahead!

Pause and Reflect

1   Do you trust that God loves you and wants your good? How is 1 Kings 6:35 one small piece of evidence that He does?

- -

2   How can we see God's love even in the daily troubles of life that are a result of the curse on creation?

OLD TESTAMENT SUMMIT

1 Kings 10:23-24: "King Solomon surpassed all the kings of the world in riches and in wisdom. The whole world wanted an audience with Solomon to hear the wisdom that God had put in his heart."

We've reached the summit of the Old Testament. All of Israel's history has been ascending toward this moment. God has blessed the nation with peace on the outside, prosperity on the inside, the respect of the nations, and His own presence.

God had told Abraham that his seed would bless the nations. Now the nations were at Solomon's doorstep asking for wisdom, asking to trade merchandise, asking the age-old question "How'd you do it?!" Answer: Solomon asked God for wisdom, and God gave it. He feared the Lord, which is the beginning of wisdom.

What's the lesson for you? God has tasked you, like Solomon, to take dominion in this world. For most people, He wants you to marry and have children and then do something with the plot of dirt in front of you, such as grow roses, build skyscrapers, arrange musical notes, pass legislation, or build a rocket to Mars (Gen. 1:26-28). Wisdom begins with recognizing that this is God's world and then representing His rule through your work. It's the "skill" of doing this well (e.g. Ex. 28:3; 31:6). So lesson one: Work and love today to create order, harmony, and peace for the good of people around you. When they turn to you and say, "How'd you do it?" give praise to God.

But there's a second lesson: Recognize that this kind of wisdom wasn't enough to keep Solomon on the mountaintop. As we will soon see, this mountain quickly crumbled. We need a deeper wisdom to bring lasting harmony and peace. Do you know who this wisdom is (see 1 Cor. 1:24)?

Pause and Reflect

1 What's your occupation? How will the fear of the Lord make you wiser in your line of work?

- -

2 Why is the wisdom of Solomon ultimately insufficient to bring lasting peace and joy to you and to others? What wisdom is needed?

DISCUSSION QUESTIONS

1   What is it in the human heart that longs for a new ruler to fix the world? That keeps rulers from bringing such lasting change?

2   What does God's decision to reign through a human being teach us about the dignity and value of humanity? What clues in these verses suggest that these promises to David ultimately point to another royal Mediator?

3   In 2 Samuel 7:11b-16, we see that everything David had came from God and everything promised would be God's doing. Who gets the credit for all of David's victories? What are some successes or accomplishments in your life for which you've wrongly taken credit? What would 1 Corinthians 4:7 say in response?

4   What do our ongoing struggles with pride, arrogance, or the need for control say about our grasp of the gospel?

5   God said that He redeemed Israel to make a great name for Himself. How is God making a great name for Himself through your life? What are some ways you try to steal fame from God? What are some ways you shape your life in order to promote His fame?

6   Why do you think Solomon felt the need to pray for God to cause us "to be devoted to Him, to walk in all His ways, and to keep His commands"? Aren't we responsible to obey regardless?

7   How should Solomon's example of prayer in verse 58 affect our prayer lives?

8   The nations around Israel were to behold the life of Israel and know there was no God but God. What does this teach us about the relationship between the life of a local church and its evangelism? How can we personally help our church's evangelism?

Chapter 8

Psalms

Songs for New Creation Hearts

Have you noticed how easily we remember commercial jingles from years ago? Here are a couple you might remember: "My bologna has a first name, it's O–S–C–A–R…" "Gimme a break, gimme a break, break me off a piece of that Kit Kat® bar." Why do these songs get stuck in our heads? For one, music helps the brain recall the words that go with the music. But also, music has a way, by God's good design, of involving our minds and hearts, our understanding and our passions.

Music engages us, and not just as individuals but as groups of people too. Listen as a college football crowd sings its fight song or as citizens sing their national anthem. Music is how human beings often unite their hearts together around memories from the past, convictions in the present, and ambitions for the future. The songs that we choose to sing have a way of revealing what our hearts most cherish, both as individuals and as groups.

We now come to Psalms and a pause in the Old Testament story line. God's covenant people used the psalms to remember God's mighty acts in their individual lives and in their national life together. Some songs offer praises. Some cry out for deliverance. Some confess sin. Some contemplate God's law. All of them give the mind and heart a language for wrestling through the challenges and joys of living in a fallen world under a magnificent God.

In this chapter, we will look briefly at four different psalms. We will see that these are songs for a new creation people. Anyone can sing college fight songs or national anthems or candy bar commercials. But the delights, confessions, celebrations, and hopes expressed in the lyrics of the psalms are truly found only in hearts indwelt by God's Holy Spirit, hearts that sing loudest of Jesus whether or not people are looking.

Psalm 1: Delighting in God's Word

1 *How happy is the man who does not follow the advice of the wicked*
or take the path of sinners
or join a group of mockers!
2 *Instead, his delight is in the LORD's instruction,*
and he meditates on it day and night.
3 *He is like a tree planted beside streams of water*
that bears its fruit in season
and whose leaf does not wither.
Whatever he does prospers.
4 *The wicked are not like this;*
instead, they are like chaff that the wind blows away.

5 *Therefore the wicked will not survive the judgment,*
and sinners will not be in the community of the righteous.
6 *For the LORD watches over the way of the righteous,*
but the way of the wicked leads to ruin.

If you are a Christian, you have probably discovered that reading God's Word can seem both delightful and dull. Sometimes it's like a glass of cold water to a parched mouth. But sometimes it looks like a big plate of brown rice without seasoning or garnish. Sure, it might be healthy, but wouldn't you prefer a pizza?

This conflict is one more piece of evidence for the battle between the old man and the new man inside of us. The new man loves God's Word. The old man thinks it tastes like cardboard. So what do we do with the word "delight" in verse 2?

Delight is a *heart* word. It's easy to think about your heart delighting in vacation or your spouse's embrace or even ice cream. But God's Word? This song envisions a person who deep down inside, in his very heart of hearts, delights, loves, cherishes, values, and longs to hear God's instruction.

Because his heart delights in it, he meditates on it day and night. He not only reads it, he leans back in his chair and lets it roll around in his head for a while. He doesn't check his e-mail or jump up to finish some task. He lets God's Word soak into his mind slowly and deliberately, almost like we do when fanaticizing about all sorts of other things.

The activity of meditating on the Bible follows the disposition of delighting in the Bible. Do you know anyone like that?

You do, actually—Jesus. And this psalm points forward to the coming King. Remember when Jesus, whose stomach was growling with hunger from 40 days of fasting, was given an opportunity by Satan to turn stones into bread? He replied, "Man must not live on bread alone but on every word that comes from the mouth of God" (Matt. 4:4). The Father's words were Jesus' meat and drink. He meditated on them day and night. And do you know what He became? He became like a tree whose fruit would feed the nations.

Psalm 1 is a song for us to sing as individual Christians and as a church, trusting not in our perfect delight in God's Word but trusting in Jesus' perfect delight in God's Word. It's also a call for us to wash ourselves continually in God's Word and to rehearse it with one another. Look at the reference to the "community of the righteous" (v. 5). God's Word is where our church will find its fight song, its national anthem, its songs for singing in the shower.

The most important thing we can do as a church is gather weekly to meditate together on God's Word through the preaching of the Word, the reading of the Word, singing the Word, and praying the Word. It's God Word that tells us who God is, who we are, and commissions our lives. It defines and shapes us as a people. It gives us life. Then having gathered to meditate on it together, we scatter to meditate on it and obey it throughout the week—day and night.

Psalm 51:1-5: Confessing Our Sin

1 *Be gracious to me, God,*
according to Your faithful love;
according to Your abundant compassion,
blot out my rebellion.
2 *Wash away my guilt and cleanse me from my sin.*
3 *For I am conscious of my rebellion,*
and my sin is always before me.
4 *Against You—You alone—I have sinned*
and done this evil in Your sight.
So You are right when You pass sentence;
You are blameless when You judge.
5 *Indeed, I was guilty when I was born;*
I was sinful when my mother conceived me.

Do you remember the story of King David's sin with Bathsheba? From the roof of his palace, David saw the beautiful Bathsheba bathing. He slept with her. She became pregnant. He had her husband killed so he could quickly marry her and try to cover over his sin. Yet God was displeased with David, and so He sent the prophet Nathan to explain that he had seen what David had done.

This psalm gives us David's response, and in this response we see how the new creation heart responds to sin. The difference between a Christian and a non-Christian is not that a Christian never sins; it's that when he does sin, he confesses it and fights against sinning again. He takes God's side against his sin instead of sin's side against God.

You can tell that Psalm 51 is the song of a new creation heart because only this kind of heart truly stops hiding and trying to justify itself. Only this kind of heart mourns sin as an offense fundamentally against God (v. 4). It's God's law that has been broken, and God's person that has been affronted, even if there's a secondary sense in which sin against Him is sin against those made in His image. And a new creation heart mourns all this, just as David truly mourned his sin.

Can you think of an occasion in which you did something wrong, and deep down you knew it was wrong, but on the surface you didn't want to admit it? Maybe it was a lie. Maybe it was your tone with your spouse. Perhaps you even tried to convince yourself that your action was not wrong.

We justify our sins by downplaying their magnitude ("It's not that bad"), shifting blame ("It's her fault"), or simply dismissing them ("I'm moving on; what's done is done!"). Inside we're like a clinched fist. We don't want to be found out as a fraud, so all our defenses are up. This is how the world responds to the charge of sin. It refuses to fess up.

But when you become a Christian and the Spirit begins to move in you, that clinched fist begins to relax. You find yourself able to confess your sin. Strangely, you feel freed. The anxiety of self-protection lifts.

How is it that a person becomes free to confess? Here's the remarkable, universe-shaking answer: Being justified before God does not depend on our righteousness but on God and His character. Look again at verse 1. The psalmist knows that it's God's faithful love and compassion that are his only hope for forgiveness, not his clean track record.

And where has God's faithful love and compassion been revealed most fully? In the death of Jesus on the cross. Jesus took upon Himself the punishment that we deserve. It's not that God simply overlooks sin. No, God is good, and so He must punish sin. But the good news is that Jesus took on that punishment so that we are now free to take the words of David into our mouths: "Wash away my guilt and cleanse me from my sin. For I am conscious of my rebellion, and my sin is always before me."

How about our hearts? Are we ready to look inside and confess the dirt or are we too bent on defending ourselves? Too stubborn to concede any territory to our spouses, our friends, our children? God is blameless when He judges (v. 4). All sin will be exposed. So why continue to hide it? Let's expose it today, trusting in His love and grace to blot out, to wash away, to cleanse. It is God who justifies, says Romans 8. Let's glory in the Mount Everest of Christ's righteousness, not in the pebbles of our good deeds.

Psalm 100: Celebrating God's Character and Work

1 *Shout triumphantly to the* LORD, *all the earth.*
2 *Serve the* LORD *with gladness;*
come before Him with joyful songs.
3 *Acknowledge that Yahweh is God.*
He made us, and we are His—
His people, the sheep of His pasture.

4 *Enter His gates with thanksgiving*
and His courts with praise.
Give thanks to Him and praise His name.
5 *For Yahweh is good, and His love is eternal;*
His faithfulness endures through all generations.

Notice *what* this psalm commands us to do (the imperative verbs): shout (v. 1), serve and come (v. 2), acknowledge (v. 3), and enter (v. 4). Notice *how* we should do these things (the adverbs): shout *triumphantly* (v. 1), serve *with gladness* and come *with joyful songs* (v. 2), enter *with thanksgiving* (v. 4).

Notice how the psalmist answers this question. He says to cast our eyes on the God of creation (v. 3) and redemption (v. 5). God is worthy of joy and triumphant shouting because He created us. Because He saved us and made us His people, the sheep of His pasture. Because He's good. Because His love is eternal. Because His faithfulness endures forever and ever, unlike the love and faithfulness we've known from any parent or friend or spouse or even ourselves.

How quickly we take for granted the fact that we are Christians! We forget how deep our sin goes, and we forget the depth of the mercy He has shown in dying on the cross and making us His sheep. In other words, our hearts *don't* shout triumphantly and we *don't* come with joy because self-righteousness and pride have crept back in. We think we deserve to be here. Or just the opposite, our pride shows itself in the fact that we don't think we deserve to be numbered among His people because we haven't proven ourselves yet.

Instead, we must remember that God has adopted us and made us His. He has rescued us. And it's this remarkable story of creation, rebellion, and then adoption that fuels our hearts to joy.

Maybe you come from a broken home and have a hard time believing that a Heavenly Father might love you so much. Maybe your home was just fine, but you're still ambitious and want to prove yourself to the world. You want the love that will come through your looks, your work, your success as a parent, your money, or your wisdom.

But God's love in Christ is so much better than anything you can earn. God doesn't say, "I love you because you're righteous…because you're pretty…because you're wise." He says, "I love you because…I love you" (see Deut. 7:7-8). He says, "I have made you mine. You are My child. I love you. All My resources of power and wisdom I pour out for your sake. What's more, I'll keep doing this because I'm faithful. I'm not fickle like people. I am devoted to you. I'll see you through to the end."

Psalm 110: Hoping in the Messiah's Victory

1 *This is the declaration of the LORD to my Lord:*
"Sit at My right hand until I make Your enemies Your footstool."
2 *The LORD will extend Your mighty scepter from Zion.*
Rule over Your surrounding enemies.
3 *Your people will volunteer on Your day of battle.*
In holy splendor, from the womb of the dawn,
the dew of Your youth belongs to You.
4 *The LORD has sworn an oath and will not take it back:*
"Forever, You are a priest like Melchizedek."
5 *The Lord is at Your right hand;*
He will crush kings on the day of His anger.
6 *He will judge the nations, heaping up corpses;*
He will crush leaders over the entire world.
7 *He will drink from the brook by the road;*
therefore, He will lift up His head.

Psalm 1 says there are two ways to live: one way leads to life; one way leads to destruction. Psalm 100 has us consider God's love for we who are His people. But in Psalm 110, we hear of the Son's victory over those who are not His people—over those who do not confess their sins as David did in Psalm 51.

We should take care not to downplay the tough words we see in this psalm. It is unloving to pretend that the judgment of Christ will be better than what the Bible says it will be. Jesus—this Priest-King in the order of Melchizedek— "will crush kings on the day of His anger. He will judge the nations, heaping up corpses" (vv. 5-6). This is a stomach-churning image, isn't it? Is this really something we should read out loud in church? We must not presume to be wiser than the Holy Spirit, who published these words. What's more, He put them in a song so that we might sing them.

And once more, it is only a new creation, Holy Spirit indwelt heart that sings of Christ's promised victory. A new creation heart looks inward and sees sin, yes. (We've talked about that in Ps. 51.) But a new creation heart also looks out at the world and sees its evil and injustice; it sees the children who abandon their parents in their old age; it sees the sexual slave trade of girls and young women; it sees the wars and acts of terror; it sees acts of economic exploitation; it sees the racial discrimination that persists in this nation and around the world; it sees the millions of aborted children. It sees all this, and the new creation heart weeps because God's laws are not kept (119:136).

The new creation heart longs for evil to be punished and for the world to be set right. It longs for justice because it knows God's justice is good and wonderful. The new creation heart trusts the judgment of God. His judgment is far better and far wiser and far more loving than our own.

Frankly, this is why movies out of Hollywood based around the theme of revenge work. This is why you want to see the bad guy get his comeuppance before the movie ends. You don't just want him arrested; you want him beat up and then arrested. Even the natural heart longs for justice. Yet it's the supernaturally indwelt heart that perceives that true justice ultimately comes from God.

Yes, Lord Jesus, judge the nations. Yes, King Jesus, crush all who opposes You and bring the hurt and death that characterize this world!

Conclusion

Half the psalms were written by David, which is why the Psalter as a whole is often associated with David. Why is this significant? Because it's David who, more than anyone else in Old Testament history, pointed people to David's greater Son—to Jesus.

The Book of Psalms was a songbook for the people of Israel. In fact, it provided Jesus with a hymnal too. In the Gospels, He quotes it more than any other Old Testament book.

Sometimes Jesus said that its verses were *about* Him, particularly when they referred to a conquering son of David. Sometimes He put its verses into His mouth as if they were *by* Him, particularly when the psalmist spoke as a suffering man. He is the happy Man of Psalm 1 who meditated on God's Word. He is the conquering Son of Psalm 2 and the victorious One with enemies under His feet in Psalm 110. But He is also the forsaken and mocked One of Psalm 22. He is the One given vinegar for His thirst in Psalm 69.

And here's some more good news for us. Since Christ came to identify Himself with a people, Psalms must finally be a songbook for Christians and churches. Jesus invites His covenant people to recite these lyrics *with* Him and always *through* Him.

Our still-sinful hearts are slow to read the psalms with all the weeping and joy the lyrics deserve. But our new creation hearts can begin to. By the power of the Spirit, we grab hold of Christ's garment as He blazes the trail. Through Christ, churches can pick up this songbook in order to praise, rejoice, mourn, confess, ask, take refuge, and hope in the mighty God of creation and redemption.

Devotions

Sleep!

In this chapter we pause in the Old Testament story line and take a look at Psalms—God's songbook for His covenant people. Take a moment to read Psalm 3.

The psalmist had learned the key to a good night's sleep. Did you notice that? "I lie down and sleep; I wake again because the LORD sustains me." Enemy forces surrounded him, but he put his trust here: "You, LORD, are a shield around me, my glory, and the One who lifts up my head." No tossing and turning for him at 3 a.m.

Enemies and anxieties fill our days too. What causes you anxiety? What fills you with fear? The Bible never promises that bad things won't happen to you. Bad things will happen, but God's people know that God will still give His glory to His redeemed ones.

In other words, fear lies to us about the significance of things. It says that the thing making you anxious is ultimate. It says that it has control of you and will determine your fate. It commands you to lie in bed and fret or not to enjoy a meal with your family because you have some serious worrying to do.

Instead of looking to our fears, we must look to our Savior. The world did its worst to Him, and yet God raised Him from the grave and gave Him a name that is above every name. Have you not been united to this beloved Son in baptism? Buried and raised again to newness of life? The Lord will save and vindicate you. So sleep! You are precious to Him. Lay down and rest, trusting the strength of His arm and the love of His heart for you.

Pause and Reflect

1 What is causing you anxiety today? How does the knowledge that you have been united to Christ in His burial and resurrection change the significance of whatever is causing you anxiety?

2 How can you encourage an anxious friend or family member with the gospel?

WHERE IS GOD?

Read Psalm 42. Notice that the psalmist asks a number of questions but they never get answered. He asks why he is depressed and suffering turmoil (v. 5). He asks why God has forgotten him and why he feels so much sorrow (v. 9). And then like an exasperated child who is not being heard, he repeats himself word for word, maybe a little bit louder: "Why am I so depressed? Why this turmoil within me?" (v. 11).

Most Christians experience such times: adversity on the outside and turmoil on the inside. You turn to God for help, but no answer comes. Nothing changes.

The psalmist's next move is instructive: "Put your hope in God, for I will still praise Him, my Savior and my God." No answer has come, but he still preaches God's salvation to himself. He doesn't grow bitter and walk away. Instead, he is like the one with childlike faith who keeps trusting even when the parent does not give the desired answer (see Matt. 18:3-4).

How is this possible? It's God that he most wants, not better circumstances in this world. Listen to the first verses again: "As a deer longs for streams of water, so I long for You, God. I thirst for God, the living God."

If difficult times come and it's not God that you really want, your heart will abandon Him because He's not giving you your true desire. But if it's God that you most want, the worst circumstances in the world are not so scary after all. You still have your heart's greatest love.

Is this not a comfort, Christian? You are a precious child of the Heavenly Father, and He is with you, even when His answer is "Not yet."

Pause and Reflect

1   What have past trials revealed about your love for God versus your love for favorable circumstances?

---

2   How does Psalm 42 prepare you for future trials?

THE REIGN OF CHRIST

Read Psalm 72. What do you think of the rule of Christ? Does it sound heavy to you, or arduous? We can be tempted into thinking of God's authority that way. But according to this psalm, consider what Christ's rule will bring: justice and righteousness; vindication for the afflicted and help for the poor; prosperity and flourishing to the earth; the obedience and worship of the nations; redemption for the oppressed and grain for the land.

Have you known anyone whose leadership brought such abundance? No wonder the psalmist erupts in praise: May He live long! May His name endure forever! May His fame increase! May all nations be blessed by Him and call Him blessed!

How strange, then, that we so easily despise the rule of Christ in our lives. Truth be told, we think we can fix whatever the problem is. A marriage? A friendship? A problem at work or church? We're confident in our ability to bring peace and justice. What's more, we want the fame and glory. May His fame increase; may gold be given to Him!—these words do not come so easily to our tongues.

But look through this psalm once more and consider how worthy of praise Christ is. His rule is like the rain that falls on the grass, like spring showers that water the earth. Do you see the budding shoots rising up? He brings life and goodness. Marvel and wonder and long for Him. He is the One for whom we are waiting. He is the One for whom we are made. He is the One who will set the disorder and injustices of your own life to right. He will heal your hurt and vindicate your faith.

Can you believe it? There exists a Man, a King, who is so good that you will want nothing more than to be near Him—to know His blessing and to call Him blessed.

Pause and Reflect

1   Can you recount some of the ways in which Christ's rule in your own life has led to your good?

- -

2   What are some of the things that tempt you to reject Christ's rule today?

DISCUSSION QUESTIONS

1   Do you ever sing with the radio in your car? Or maybe in the shower? When you do, do you find yourself becoming more spirited than you would be if someone were watching? What is it about music that engages us this way?

2   What do the songs we sing communicate about who we are and what we value? What songs does your heart most naturally sing? What do you and the people closest to you sing?

3   How does the knowledge that we cannot fully live according to the wise path laid out in Psalm 1 drive us to the gospel?

4   In what ways can you prioritize reading God's Word in your daily schedule? How important is it to read the Bible with your family? With your church?

5   What are some of the excuses we give to justify our sins? In what ways do we seek to blame others for our sins?

6   How can we as a body of believers challenge one another to be more open to quick confession of sin? Why is it important for vertical confession (to God) to lead to horizontal confession (to others)? In what ways can we who have been shown mercy extend God's mercy to others?

7   Psalm 100 talks about heart attitudes: Don't just come, come with joy. But what if we're not feeling joy? Do we talk ourselves into it? What should we do when we know our heart should respond in praise and joy but instead we seem cold to God's truth?

8   What is the connection between celebration of God's work and involvement in God's mission? Why is it important that evangelism be the overflow of worshipful hearts?

9   In what ways do the psalms help form our prayers so that our hearts' desires align with God's heart?

10 How does our understanding of future justice motivate the Christian's efforts to relieve temporal suffering and work for justice in the present?

Chapter 9

Wisdom

Its Role in the Lives of God's People

VOICES FROM *Church History*

"Except a man fear the Lord, he is unable to renounce sin." [1]
–Ambrose (circa 340-397)

VOICES FROM *Church History*

"Though Satan should buffet, though trials should come, Let this blest assurance control, That Christ has regarded my helpless estate, And hath shed His own blood for my soul."
–Horatio Spafford (1828-1888), "It Is Well with My Soul"

Imagine being lost at sea in a boat with two other people. Your compass has fallen into the water. You don't know if you're facing north or south, east or west. You have good sails and the craft is seaworthy, but you don't know where to guide the boat.

Night falls, and one of your fellow shipmates excitedly points to a bright point of light in the sky—the North Star. He tells you he knows how to navigate by the stars. But your other shipmate says the idea of navigating by the stars is ridiculous and that she has a positive sense of which way to sail—an "internal compass," she calls it. Now they are calling on you to decide whom to follow. Your vote decides who will direct the boat. Which leader will you choose?

Every day, we encounter situations that confront us with important decisions. These situations bring up questions that require wisdom—the skill of making your way safely to harbor amidst choppy waters. Questions such as: "My boss asks me to tell people on the phone that he's not in the office. But I don't want to lie. What should I say?" "How should we discipline our children?" "They were such an amazing family! Why did God take their lives in a car accident?" "He cheats on his wife and is the world's biggest liar. But he's rich, healthy, and happy. How is that fair?" "He's a godly man and clearly loves me. Should I marry him?" "How much time should I spend with my children versus working to provide for them?"

Here we look at several Old Testament wisdom literature texts, specifically Job, Proverbs, Ecclesiastes, and Song of Songs. Biblical wisdom is the skill of living successfully in God's created but fallen world. Wisdom is concerned with the nature of reality and whether you can skillfully bring order and navigate your way through it. Wisdom literature helps us learn how to live in light of eternity and points forward to Jesus Christ, our wisdom.

Wisdom is rooted in the fear of God (Prov. 1:7).

7 *The fear of the* LORD
is the beginning of knowledge;
fools despise wisdom and discipline.

Wisdom is rooted in the fear of God. Or to use the illustration of being lost at sea, wisdom finds its single most important coordinate—its absolute standard by which all else is measured—in the fear of God. The word "knowledge" here is being used synonymously with "wisdom," which is what fools hate, as you can see from the last line. The fear of the Lord, this verse teaches us, is the North Star that helps us determine which way to sail. Without God and the knowledge that all of life is lived under God's rule, we are completely lost at sea.

"The fear of the LORD" is not exactly the same thing as being afraid, but in a sense, it's not less either (see Matt. 10:28). It's the recognition that God is your Creator, Ruler, and Judge and that all of life is lived under His eye. It's the recognition that He created you for Himself and that He has promised to bless all those who trust and follow Him and to curse all those who do not. Each of us has a choice: We can try to guide ourselves by some internal compass or we can let the "North Star" guide us.

How do you honor yet say no to your boss when he asks you to lie? How do you respond to life's tragedies? How should we respond to the prosperity of the wicked? Should you marry this person or that person? Take this job or that job? Why is it so difficult to be disciplined with your personal devotions?

You need the answers that will guide you to safe harbor, and you want the skill of finding those answers. You want it for your spouse's sake, your children's sake, your friend and fellow church member's sake. For your sake. You want wisdom. So get wisdom! How? By fearing the Lord. Recognize that *everything* in life must be measured in relation to Him as to the North Star—from your words to your boss to how you respond to tragedy and suffering.

The fool is the one who insists on going his own way. That's why living according to the wisdom of the world, we say things such as "I'm just expressing myself" or "I need to be true to myself" or "I love him and love is never wrong" or "I'm just being real."

Do you see what's behind these kinds of phrases? A person's internal desires are pitted against outward instruction or constraint, and the internal state is treated as "more real" and "more morally legitimate" than any outside word.

The wisdom of the age is "Be true to yourself," and certainly God has given every individual unique gifts and perspectives. But apart from the guiding light of the "North Star"—the fear of the Lord—this devolves into complete folly. Then does living wisely mean living without passion? Not at all, as we are about to see.

Wisdom directs our passions (Song of Sg. 6:3).

Wisdom doesn't mean living without passion. It means living with *directed* passions. We learn this especially in the Song of Songs. Take a look at this well-known verse from the Bible's most extended love poem:

3 *I am my love's and my love is mine.*

She is his, and he is hers—forever. Their love is an exclusive love. That is, their love is constrained—constrained to exclusivity. It's channeled like water through a canal. Each lover gives love with all its enjoyments to the other person and to no other. Along the way, threats come to this love—guards come and threaten the woman (5:7); people ask why she loves him and not some other (5:9). But amidst the challenges, their love remains strong and fixed upon one another.

This is exactly what God's Word is celebrating in this poem—the fires and passions of marital love: "For love is as strong as death; ardent love is as unrelenting as Sheol. Love's flames are fiery flames—the fiercest of all. Mighty waters cannot extinguish love; rivers cannot sweep it away" (8:6-7).

Do you see how powerful love is? Once set in motion, it's nearly unstoppable, like mighty flood waters. Many of us know from our own experience how powerful love can be. But our culture fails to recognize that it's the very strength of love that requires us to be careful with it. Water is surely good, but water unleashed is destructive. Three times the poem warns, "Do not stir up or awaken love until the appropriate time" (2:7; 3:5; 8:4).

Love can surely be foolish and wrong. We too easily love the wrong things and too easily love in the wrong ways. This is why Jesus never separates love and obedience (John 14:15,21). Our culture believes not that God is love but that love is a god. It makes an idol out of love, as many of the love songs on the radio and romance movies in the theater testify. It believes you can always justify some action or lifestyle by calling it "loving" and that nothing should constrain love— not God's law, not God's wisdom.

This is why biblical wisdom is so desperately needed. Wisdom recognizes that fallen humans can take a good thing and pervert it, like love. So wisdom channels our passions into life-giving canals. It channels the energy of a five-year-old into activity on the playground instead of fighting with a sibling. It channels a passion for justice into a legal career instead of revenge. It channels a passion for cooking into hospitality for fellow church members instead of gluttony. In other words, wisdom takes the raw energies and emotions and affections that come with being human and directs them in a life-giving path.

Again, think of the boat sitting in the middle of the ocean. Which way is the right way to go? A person might feel deeply passionate that the boat should turn *this* way. But without wisdom to guide it, what are the chances that this deep passion will guide the boat in the right direction?

The beauty of God's wisdom is that He has made us with passions and has given us His wise Word to guide those passions. The Song of Songs is a perfect example: it places the diamond of marital love into the platinum prongs of wisdom.

Wisdom provides the proper perspective on life in a fallen world (Job 1:20-21).

It's important to know that the Bible's wisdom literature *often* works by pointing out what's *proverbially* true. A proverbial truth is a general truth, not a scientific or mathematic truth. It's proverbially true that the early bird gets the worm. But one morning, it could be that the lazy bird who sleeps in gets the worm while the early bird cannot find a worm.

The Book of Proverbs is filled with such proverbial truths. It's a kind of wisdom that looks at the world as God intended it at creation. It's the kind of wisdom you teach to your children. You teach them to work hard. You teach them to listen. You teach them to avoid temptation. And such proverbial wisdom says that when you do these things, you will prosper.

This is how the world should work. It's built on the sowing/reaping principle, which itself is built on cause and effect. Work hard and your barn will be full. Sleep through the harvest and you will go hungry. Sow—reap. Cause—effect. This is the world as God created it. And this is the path of wisdom that we as Christians should especially pursue.

Yet life isn't always so simple. This world is fallen and broken, and things don't always go as they should. Of course, the wisdom literature recognizes exactly this: "'Absolute futility,' says the Teacher. 'Absolute futility. Everything is futile.' What does a man gain for all his efforts that he labors at under the sun?" (Eccl. 1:2-3). "The Teacher" goes on to say everyone dies. So why be wise instead of foolish?

Fools achieve political power, while princes labor as slaves. The righteous man perishes in his righteousness, while the wicked man prolongs his life in his evildoing. So why be righteous? Why listen to the father in Proverbs or try to love your wife as portrayed in the Song of Songs?

With this tension between the moral principles and the hard realities looming in the background, we must remember a third lesson about wisdom. Wisdom, we said, provides the proper perspective on life in a fallen and broken world. It provides a proper perspective on what seems like a breakdown in the sowing/reaping principle. Take the words of Job. This wealthy man had just encountered great tragedy in his own life, including the loss of his children, his household staff, and his large herds of livestock. Yet his response was to acknowledge the Lord's hand in giving and removing and then to praise the Lord.

20 *Then Job stood up, tore his robe, and shaved his head. He fell to the ground and worshiped,* 21 *saying:*
Naked I came from my mother's womb,
and naked I will leave this life.
The LORD gives, and the LORD takes away.
Praise the name of Yahweh.

If the fear of the Lord is the beginning of wisdom, then wisdom teaches us that the Lord is in charge of everything, as the final few chapters of Job affirm ever so clearly. The Bible does not give us the ability to explain away the problem of evil. We only need to affirm that He alone is God, that He alone is to be feared, not natural disasters or financial meltdowns or unjust bosses, and that He gives and takes away as He pleases. The wise person affirms this. The fool, like Job's wife, resists it.

The fear of the Lord must remain our North Star when the seas are stormy and when they are calm. Again this comes through loud and clear in Job 38 when God says to Job, "Where were you when I established the earth?" (v. 4). That is, "I am God. You are not. Are you capable of trusting Me even when you don't understand? If not, if you always demand an explanation to your satisfaction, then it would seem that you are adamant about being God."

Wisdom guides our priorities and points us to Christ (Eccl. 12:13-14).

What's wonderful about Scripture is how realistic it is. Karl Marx called religion the opiate of the masses. He regarded it as a way for people to anesthetize themselves to the pain of living. But the Bible doesn't do this. It stares right into the face of suffering and pain, taking a more honest look than Marx ever did.

This should comfort us as Christians because it tells us that the pains, trials, and injustices we experience are not unexpected. The Lord knows our trials, and He allows them for our good. The final chapter of Ecclesiastes begins with a litany of bad things that will take place in one's life. So the author says before suffering comes your way, *remember your Creator.* He is the North Star who gives us our coordinates, who orients our lives and instructs our paths. Ecclesiastes ends this way:

13 *When all has been heard, the conclusion of the matter is: fear God and keep His commands, because this is for all humanity.* 14 *For God will bring every act to judgment, including every hidden thing, whether good or evil.*

We're back to where we started. God is the Judge of all things. So fear Him before all else. Keep His commands. Even when life seems difficult and excuses for disobedience lie close at hand, obey Him. The wise in heart make a priority of obeying God because the wise in heart know He alone is to be feared.

Does all this mean wisdom saves us? That depends on what you mean. Will the attempt to fear the Lord and keep His commands save you? No, because no matter how hard we try, all of us have fallen short of the glory of God. Wisdom cannot save you just as the law cannot save you.

But there is another sense in which wisdom does indeed save. Wisdom is a Person, and His name is Jesus. Jesus Himself tells us, "[the queen of the south] came from the ends of the earth to hear the wisdom of Solomon; and look— something greater than Solomon is here!" (Matt. 12:42).

Jesus is the perfectly dutiful Son who listens to His Father's words: "I have not come to speak My words but the words of Him who sent Me" (see John 12:49). Jesus lived righteously and wisely according to the cause-and-effect principles of sowing and reaping. Christ is the creation wisdom of God in whom are hidden all the treasures of wisdom and knowledge (see Col. 1:15-18; 2:3).

Yet Jesus is the wisdom of God in another sense. Like Job, Jesus receives the curses of the fool in the wisdom literature. He lived in poverty and died a criminal, cut off in the prime of His life. He was scorned and mocked, beaten and abandoned by His friends, and finally killed.

But it's precisely this vein of thought that leads Paul to refer to the cross as the wisdom of God. Listen to 1 Corinthians 1:18,24: "For the message of the cross is foolishness to those who are perishing…Yet to those who are called, both Jews and Greeks, Christ is God's power and God's wisdom."

Christ is the Creator who, in His wisdom, breathed the universe into being and holds it together. And Christ is the Redeemer who, through His death and resurrection, defeated the very things that the books of Job and Ecclesiastes say bring futility to creation: sin and death.

The Book of Ecclesiastes calls everything under the sun meaningless and futile. Well, sure that might be true for living under the sun of the old creation. But what about the new creation brought about by Christ's resurrection?

The world calls this foolishness, both because it doesn't believe in the resurrection and because it doesn't understand what happened on the cross. The world says you don't defeat strength with weakness, hate with love, rebellion with mercy and grace, and you certainly do not defeat death with another death. Worship a man on a cross? Are you crazy? Ah, but praise God—His foolishness is wiser than man's wisdom!

The apostle Paul taught that as believers, Christ is our wisdom: "But it is from Him that you are in Christ Jesus, who became God-given wisdom for us—our righteousness, sanctification, and redemption" (1 Cor. 1:30).

What does the fear of the Lord look like in the language of the New Testament? It looks like repentance and belief, trusting that Christ is our righteousness, sanctification, and redemption. Do you want to be skilled at navigating safely to safe harbor? Do you want to be wise? Then look to Christ.

Conclusion

We've seen how wisdom is rooted in the fear of the Lord and points us to Jesus. But wisdom doesn't stop there. It points us to others as well. In 2 Corinthians 5:10-11, Paul writes: "For we must all appear before the tribunal of Christ, so that each may be repaid for what he has done in the body, whether good or worthless. Therefore, because we know the fear of the Lord, we seek to persuade people."

In other words, living in wisdom leads to evangelism. We know the truth about God, ourselves, and the world we live in. Compelled by Christ's love and guided by Scripture's wisdom, we seek to persuade people to trust in Christ. Wisdom looks to Christ and points others to Him as well.

- -

HYMN OF *Response*

"To us the voice of Wisdom cries, Hearken, ye children, and be wise;
Better than gold the fruit I bear, Rubies to me may not compare."

"Happy the man who daily waits To hear me, watching at my gates;
Wretched is he who scorns my voice, Death and destruction are his choice."

"To them that love me I am kind; And those who seek me early find;
My Son, give me thine heart,—and learn Wisdom from folly to discern."

"Mark, the beginning of my law, —Fear ye the Lord with sacred awe;
Mark the fulfilment of the whole, Love ye the Lord with all your soul."

"We hear, we learn; may we obey; Jesus, the life, the truth, the way,
Wisdom and righteousness, we see, Grace and salvation all in Thee."
–James Montgomery, "To Us the Voice of Wisdom Cries"

- -

Devotions

TEACHABILITY

Proverbs 9:8: "Don't rebuke a mocker, or he will hate you; rebuke a wise man, and he will love you."

One of the greatest virtues a person can cultivate through God's grace is teachability. Teachability is the opposite of pride. Pride has nothing to learn and is the path of the fool. But the humble person, the person whom God favors, is teachable. His or her knee-jerk response to criticism is not to say, "I'm the expert, not you." Those who are teachable search for wisdom as for hidden treasure, and they are happy to find it in the most unexpected places.

Who are the most teachable people? Those who understand the gospel. They are not gripped with the need to justify, defend, or prove themselves. Instead, they know their justification is found in the righteousness, worth, and beauty of Christ. They are like a kid on the playground who is happy to walk amidst the bullies because his body-building brother walks by his side. Standing in the safe shadow of our "older Brother," the gospel believer feels free to say, "I have a lot to learn. I make mistakes. Teach me."

Was Jesus teachable? Luke tells us that Jesus "increased in wisdom and stature" (Luke 2:52). Isaiah says that He awoke "each morning...to listen like those being instructed" (Isa. 50:4). Though being in nature God, Jesus exemplified teachability (see John 14:10). How much more should we?

Do you want to become someone people trust? Cultivate teachability. Are you looking for a delightful spouse? Find someone who is teachable. Do you want to grow as a leader? Become teachable. Do you want, most importantly, to look like Jesus? Then trust Jesus' perfect justifying work for you, and then follow in His footsteps.

Pause and Reflect

1   In your own words, how will embracing Jesus' unique work in His death and resurrection help you become more teachable?

---

2   What are some relationships in which you should grow in teachability?

PURSUING THE WIND

Ecclesiastes 2:11: "When I considered all that I had accomplished and what I had labored to achieve, I found everything to be futile and a pursuit of the wind. There was nothing to be gained under the sun."

Ever since God cursed the ground following Adam's sin, futility has afflicted our work. You build a house; age overtakes it. You write a memo; no one reads it. You pass legislation; your successor changes it. The Book of Ecclesiastes stares right into this ugly face and names it for what it is—a pursuit of the wind.

In response to such teaching, Christians often fall into one of two errors. Error one is to work with despondency: "It's all a waste of time. Why even care?" Those who reach the very top of the professional food chain can respond this way, like the author of Ecclesiastes, but it's probably more common among those on the bottom half. Error two is to ignore this teaching and over-exalt work—to act as if we're building God's promised future world now. This is probably more common among those who are professionally successful and who hope to do even better.

But Jesus calls us to the middle road of faith. This is the road where we produce visible things with our hands but trust that it's the invisible realities that last (Col. 3:23-24). Taking the middle road of faith means acknowledging both that the clay jar you just made will break and that God will accomplish something eternal with that jar (see 2 Cor. 4:7).

What do we specifically take from Ecclesiastes' emphasis? Don't make an idol of your work because it won't get you very far. Instead, work out of rest, the rest that's found in the lasting work of Christ.

Pause and Reflect

1   How are both errors described above a consequence of idolatry?

2   How are you tempted to idolize work? What's the solution?

ONE GREATER THAN SOLOMON

Ephesians 3:8,10: "This grace was given to me—the least of all the saints—to proclaim to the Gentiles the incalculable riches of the Messiah…This is so God's multi-faceted wisdom may now be made known through the church to the rulers and authorities in the heavens."

At the height of King Solomon's reign, the prosperity and peace of his nation put his unequaled wisdom on display for the world. Foreign heads of state sought his instruction and stumbled over themselves to broker deals with him.

But now One greater than Solomon has come; He is the very wisdom of God—Jesus Christ. And the wisdom of God in Christ is put on display in the church, even the local church, where Jews and Gentiles, slaves and freemen, men and women come together as one. It's where the walls that ordinarily divide human beings fall flat.

To put it another way, the local church is where two human beings who would otherwise be enemies learn to love one another. After all, sin makes all people natural-born enemies (think of Adam blaming Eve or Cain killing Abel). It makes everyone his or her own god, which means the world is a battleground of gods. When Christ reconciles a person to Himself, He by definition reconciles that person to the whole family. So peace ensues. Old enemies now love. "By this all people will know that you are My disciples, if you have love for one another" (John 13:35).

When the world beholds your local church, what should it see? It should see a world of relationships more prosperous and peaceful than anything the Queen of Sheba ever beheld in the nation of Israel. It should see the very wisdom of God in Christ. What a privilege it is to belong to one of Christ's churches!

Pause and Reflect

1 What's the source of peace and vitality in a church? What do failures of peace indicate?

- -

2 How can you help your church grow in peace and vitality?

DISCUSSION QUESTIONS

1   How would you define "wisdom"? How does your definition differ from wisdom according to the Bible?

2   What characteristics describe a "wise" person? What are the consequences of being "unskilled" when it comes to wisdom?

3   What comes to mind when you think of "the fear of the LORD"? Is this the same as being afraid of God? Why or why not?

4   One proverb says: "There is a way that seems right to a man, but its end is the way to death" (14:12). Have you ever been in a situation in which a particular decision or path seemed so right but later you discovered it was the wrong path?

5   Can love ever be foolish and wrong? When? Under what circumstances?

6   How would you respond to a friend who says life is meaningless and therefore wisdom is of no value?

7   How should we respond to the seeming discrepancy between the moral principles of Proverbs and the hard realities of Job and Ecclesiastes?

8   How is fear of judgment one of the ways God mercifully preserves us from making sinful choices or living with misguided priorities?

9   What does biblical wisdom have to say to both the old and the young?

10 What priorities in your life would change if you began to apply godly wisdom? What priorities in your church would change?

Part 3

God's Covenant People Divided, Scattered, and Brought Back

Despite God's faithfulness, patience, and abundant covenant blessings, sin and idolatry marked His people. So God once again exiled man, but not without hope. A faithful remnant remained, and God promised restoration, even a new covenant that would address the sin and idolatry of their hearts. God brought His people back to the land, but they still longed for the further deliverance to come.

Chapter 10

Israel

The Decline and Fall of the Northern Kingdom

VOICES FROM *Church History*

"There is nothing so abominable in the eyes of God and man as idolatry, because it renders to the creature the honor that is due to none but the Creator."[1]
–Blaise Pascal (1623-1662)

VOICES FROM *Church History*

"If any occupation or association is found to hinder our communion with God or our enjoyment of spiritual things, then it must be abandoned."[2]
–A. W. Pink (1886-1952)

Everyone worships something. We might not bow down before marble idols or animal statues. But every one of us elevates something in our lives to the status of "god." Some worship sports; others worship the reputations they carefully craft online. Some worship entertainment; others money. Even atheists, who claim that God doesn't exist, elevate their ideas and demonstrate an over-reliance on their own intellects and rational capabilities. The question is not *if* we are worshiping; the question is *what* we are worshiping.

The God of the Bible describes Himself as "jealous"—"I, the LORD your God, am a jealous God" (Ex. 20:5). Moses attested to this attribute of God when he compared the Lord to a consuming fire. God is not to be trifled with.

Moses would know. When Moses climbed up to talk with God on Mount Sinai, the Israelites constructed a golden calf out of melted jewelry. They danced around it and sacrificed animals to it. They even declared it was the god who brought them out of slavery in Egypt. In His discipline of His people for their idolatry, God's fiery jealousy was on full display.

When Moses came down to the camp, the party came to a halt. He threw down the calf, burned it with fire, ground it to powder, mixed it with water, and forced the Israelites to drink the sludge. God said to Moses, "I have seen this people, and they are indeed a stiff-necked people. Now leave Me alone, so that My anger can burn against them and I can destroy them" (32:9-10). Moses interceded on Israel's behalf, and Israel was spared. Still, the Israelites discovered that God doesn't play second fiddle, never has and never will. If His people played with the fire of idolatry, they were going to get burned. And throughout the Old Testament, the people of God continually learned this lesson the hard way.

Under the wise reign of King Solomon, it seemed that the promises of God to His people were finally coming true. God's people were in the promised land, assured of His presence through the temple, and at peace under the reign of the king. But Solomon turned his heart away from God. He engaged in idol worship, and after his death, the kingdom was split in two: the Northern Kingdom (Israel) and the Southern Kingdom (Judah).

Here we will examine the decline and fall of the Northern Kingdom. God demonstrated His covenant love by raising up prophets (such as Elijah) to call His people back to a relationship with Him. But because the Northern Kingdom persisted in their rebellion, God upheld His justice by scattering the tribes among the nations. What can we learn from Israel's mistake? How can we demote existing idols? By exploring Israel's idolatry, we will be able to answer these questions. Moving forward, ask God to show you the idols in your life, and then pray for the strength to put them in their proper place.

The faithful embrace God's Word and abandon their idols (1 Kings 18:20-39).

20 *So Ahab summoned all the Israelites and gathered the prophets at Mount Carmel.* 21 *Then Elijah approached all the people and said, "How long will you hesitate between two opinions? If Yahweh is God, follow Him. But if Baal, follow him." But the people didn't answer him a word.*

22 *Then Elijah said to the people, "I am the only remaining prophet of the* LORD, *but Baal's prophets are 450 men.* 23 *Let two bulls be given to us. They are to choose one bull for themselves, cut it in pieces, and place it on the wood but not light the fire. I will prepare the other bull and place it on the wood but not light the fire.* 24 *Then you call on the name of your god, and I will call on the name of Yahweh. The God who answers with fire, He is God." All the people answered, "That sounds good."*

25 *Then Elijah said to the prophets of Baal, "Since you are so numerous, choose for yourselves one bull and prepare it first. Then call on the name of your god but don't light the fire."* 26 *So they took the bull that he gave them, prepared it, and called on the name of Baal from morning until noon, saying, "Baal, answer us!" But there was no sound; no one answered. Then they danced, hobbling around the altar they had made.*

27 *At noon Elijah mocked them. He said, "Shout loudly, for he's a god! Maybe he's thinking it over; maybe he has wandered away; or maybe he's on the road. Perhaps he's sleeping and will wake up!"* 28 *They shouted loudly, and cut themselves with knives and spears, according to their custom, until blood gushed over them.* 29 *All afternoon they kept on raving until the offering of the evening sacrifice, but there was no sound; no one answered, no one paid attention.*

30 *Then Elijah said to all the people, "Come near me." So all the people approached him. Then he repaired the* LORD's *altar that had been torn down:* 31 *Elijah took 12 stones—according to the number of the tribes of the sons of Jacob, to whom the word of the* LORD *had come, saying, "Israel will be your name"—* 32 *and he built an altar with the stones in the name of Yahweh. Then he made a trench around the altar large enough to hold about four gallons.* 33 *Next, he arranged the wood, cut up the bull, and placed it on the wood. He said, "Fill four water pots with water and pour it on the offering to be burned and on the wood."* 34 *Then he said, "A second time!" and they did it a second time. And then he said, "A third time!" and they did it a third time.* 35 *So the water ran all around the altar; he even filled the trench with water.*

36 At the time for offering the evening sacrifice, Elijah the prophet approached the altar and said, "Yahweh, God of Abraham, Isaac, and Israel, today let it be known that You are God in Israel and I am Your servant, and that at Your word I have done all these things. 37 Answer me, LORD! Answer me so that this people will know that You, Yahweh, are God and that You have turned their hearts back."

38 Then Yahweh's fire fell and consumed the burnt offering, the wood, the stones, and the dust, and it licked up the water that was in the trench. 39 When all the people saw it, they fell facedown and said, "Yahweh, He is God! Yahweh, He is God!"

On March 8, 1971, two of the greatest boxers in the world faced off in what was known as the "Fight of the Century." On one side of the ring stood Muhammad Ali. Standing in the other corner was Joe Frazier, also known as "Smokin' Joe." After 15 grueling rounds, Frazier won the fight by decision and dealt Ali his first professional loss. It was estimated that 300 million people around the world watched the fight.

Almost three thousand years prior, another showdown captivated a crowd. On one side, you had Elijah—his name meant "Yahweh is my God"—a prophet who believed that the God of the Hebrews was the only true God. On the other side, you had Ahab, king over the Northern Kingdom of Israel. Ahab worshiped Baal, the pagan god of rain and fertility.

When the two squared off on Mount Carmel, Elijah said to the crowd, "How long will you hesitate between two opinions? If Yahweh is God, follow Him. But if Baal, follow him." When the audience didn't respond, Elijah set the rules for the showdown. Whichever deity could burn up the bull on the altar would be worshiped as the one true God. It was a challenge of biblical proportions, and there could only be one winner.

After 450 prophets failed to summon Baal, Elijah began to taunt them. "Shout loudly," he said, "for he's a god! Maybe he's thinking it over; maybe he has wandered away; or maybe he's on the road. Perhaps he's sleeping and will wake up!" But no fire fell from heaven for the prophets of Baal.

When it was Elijah's turn, he boldly dug a trench around the sacrifice and filled the trench with water. Elijah wanted to make sure that the sacrifice was soaking wet so that when the fire came, the prophets of Baal and the audience would have no doubt that it was a miraculous act of God. Elijah poured water on the sacrifice three times until the moat was full. Then Elijah did something unexpected—he stepped *toward* the altar to pray (v. 36).

Perhaps Elijah stepped *toward* the altar as a way of placing his own life in God's hands. He believed God would do an amazing miracle, and Elijah wanted to see it up close.

Take another look at Elijah's prayer (vv. 36-37). Notice that Elijah did not pray for himself. He did not pray that *his* name would be upheld or that *his* reputation would come out on top. Instead, he prayed that God would receive credit for this miracle. In this way, Elijah's prayer resembled the prayers of Moses, Joshua, David, and Solomon. Even though Elijah could have been humiliated, he trusted in the power of God.

And suddenly, God answered Elijah's prayer. Fire fell from heaven and consumed the altar and the bull. Even the water Elijah had doused all over the altar evaporated. Then Elijah dealt a final blow to the prophets of Baal by having them all killed, in keeping with the law of Deuteronomy 13:1-11. It was a showdown that none could soon forget.

What do Elijah's actions teach us today? First, they teach us that God is a jealous God. When it comes to God's centrality, there can be no competition. He is the first and the last, the beginning and the end. But there is another lesson we can learn from Elijah's victory over the prophets of Baal. Elijah shows us the importance of dethroning the idols in our lives—sometimes even with drastic measures.

Jesus once said, "If your right eye causes you to sin, gouge it out and throw it away" (Matt. 5:29). What was Jesus really saying? Was He advocating self-mutilation? No. He was trying to show His disciples that God takes sin seriously. If we idolize our eyes by using them to sin against God, we need to do anything and everything in our power to de-elevate them and raise our gaze back to God. Jesus implies that blindness is better than offering continual sacrifices to false idols.

The unfaithful abandon God's Word and embrace their idols (2 Kings 17:6-18).

6 *In the ninth year of Hoshea, the king of Assyria captured Samaria. He deported the Israelites to Assyria and settled them in Halah and by the Habor, Gozan's river, and in the cities of the Medes.* 7 *This disaster happened because the people of Israel had sinned against the LORD their God who had brought them out of the land of Egypt from the power of Pharaoh king of Egypt and because they had worshiped other gods.* 8 *They had lived according to the customs of the nations that the LORD had dispossessed before the Israelites and the customs the kings of Israel had introduced.* 9 *The Israelites secretly did what was not right against the LORD their God. They built high places in all their*

towns from watchtower to fortified city. 10 They set up for themselves sacred pillars and Asherah poles on every high hill and under every green tree. 11 They burned incense on all the high places just like those nations that the LORD had driven out before them. They did evil things, provoking the LORD. 12 They served idols, although the LORD had told them, "You must not do this." 13 Still, the LORD warned Israel and Judah through every prophet and every seer, saying, "Turn from your evil ways and keep My commands and statutes according to all the law I commanded your ancestors and sent to you through My servants the prophets."

14 But they would not listen. Instead they became obstinate like their ancestors who did not believe the LORD their God. 15 They rejected His statutes and His covenant He had made with their ancestors and the decrees He had given them. They pursued worthless idols and became worthless themselves, following the surrounding nations the LORD had commanded them not to imitate.

16 They abandoned all the commands of the LORD their God. They made cast images for themselves, two calves, and an Asherah pole. They worshiped the whole heavenly host and served Baal. 17 They made their sons and daughters pass through the fire and practiced divination and interpreted omens. They devoted themselves to do what was evil in the LORD's sight and provoked Him.

18 Therefore, the LORD was very angry with Israel, and He removed them from His presence. Only the tribe of Judah remained.

According to the medical community, amnesia is a condition in which one's memory is lost. There are many types of amnesia: anterograde amnesia—the loss of short-term memory; retrograde amnesia—the loss of most or all previous memories. There is post-traumatic amnesia, dissociative amnesia, and even lacunar amnesia—or the loss of memory concerning a specific event or experience.

Throughout her history, Israel frequently suffered from amnesia. She had forgotten her history. She had forgotten the God who had delivered her from the hand of Pharaoh. She had forgotten the 10 plagues that Yahweh rained down on the Egyptians. She had forgotten how God made the Red Sea part so the Israelites could pass through the waters on dry sand and how God provided water to flow from rocks in the wilderness and manna to feed them while they wandered toward the promised land. God's people had lost the memory of Jericho and how the walls came tumbling down and how the

Lord gave victory to His people when they went to war against the Canaanites. And now in 2 Kings 17, they had once again forgotten the God who hurled fire down from heaven to consume the sacrifice of Elijah.

Throughout the Old Testament, God's people are constantly being called to remember. In Joshua 4:1-7, God told Joshua to instruct the 12 tribes of Israel to place stones in the middle of the Jordan and on the land so future generations might forever remember what God accomplished at that location. Before the Israelites entered the promised land, Moses was very clear about how and what they were to remember. He told them to "be careful not to forget the LORD who brought [them] out of the land of Egypt, out of the place of slavery" (Deut. 6:12). If anyone knew how prone to spiritual amnesia God's people were, surely it was Moses. So he encouraged them to pay attention to their history so that in the future they would not repeat the mistakes they had committed in the past.

Many generations later, the Israelites chose not to listen to the Lord, so the Lord sent fire from heaven once again. In 722 B.C., the Assyrians, ruthless and cruel, burned down the cities in the Northern Kingdom and took the people as their prisoners. Because of their disobedience, God's people learned the hard way that God meant what He said in Exodus 20:4-5: "Do not make an idol for yourself, whether in the shape of anything in the heavens above or on the earth below or in the waters under the earth. You must not bow down to them or worship them; for I, the LORD your God, am a jealous God, punishing the children for the fathers' sin, to the third and fourth generations of those who hate Me."

Because the Israelites returned to the worship of Baal, God disciplined the nation He had set His affection on. Because they had broken their allegiance to Yahweh and had practiced pagan worship rituals, God drew them back to Himself through the use of foreign armies.

Israel had lost her distinctiveness from the surrounding nations, so much so that the Israelites even offered human sacrifices to idols. God's patience had run out, and He used the Assyrian army to show His people that the covenant of blessings and curses in Deuteronomy 28:15-16 still applied: "But if you do not obey the LORD your God by carefully following all His commands and statutes I am giving you today, all these curses will come and overtake you: You will be cursed in the city and cursed in the country."

The psalmist says, "I will remember the LORD's works; yes, I will remember Your ancient wonders. I will reflect on all You have done and meditate on Your actions" (Ps. 77:11-12). Have you ever equated memory with worship?

Memory can be worshipful when we, like the psalmist, remember the mighty acts that God has accomplished. When we remember God's acts, we remember His faithfulness. When we remember His faithfulness, we remember the greatest act of faithfulness in history—Jesus Christ gave His life so you and I can forever bask in the eternal presence of God.

Jesus knew that we would suffer from spiritual amnesia, and that's why He gave us a tangible reminder: "And He took bread, gave thanks, broke it, gave it to them, and said, 'This is My body, which is given for you. Do this in remembrance of Me'" (Luke 22:19).

Conclusion

The church has always oscillated between two things: becoming like the world (syncretism) and separating from the world we are called to reach (separatism). Back and forth the pendulum swings, from one side to the other. Both affect our mission to represent Christ in the world. Syncretism makes us like the world, which dilutes our witness. Separatism removes us from the world, which keeps us from being salt and light.

In the Old Testament, God instructed His people to be separate from the practices and beliefs of the other nations. He told them to worship one God instead of many. He showed them through mighty acts of power that He alone is the only true God and that they were not to bow down to false idols. He even warned them against marrying the women of other nations because He knew the Israelites would soon adopt their idols.

Where do you fall on the scale of syncretism to separatism? How similar are your interests to those of the world? How different do your life and priorities look than those of your non-Christian family and friends?

We have seen that God takes idolatry seriously. We've seen what happens when God's people suffer from spiritual amnesia. The good news is that even when God's people are slow to repent, His love is so overwhelmingly generous that God extends the message of salvation to other nations.

Everyone worships something. Jesus Christ is the only One worthy of worship (see Rev. 5:8-9). He is the only One worth bowing to. And each day, every one of us is given a choice similar to the one Elijah gave the Israelites on Mount Carmel. The choice is yours to make. God or idols. Life or death. What will you choose?

Devotions

SEEING THE EFFECTS

Idolatry has a funny way of becoming a huge deal—a hugely messy, disruptive, and unwelcome deal. Idolatry is the unwanted house guest who, though initially invited in, overstays her welcome and ends up wreaking havoc on the entire household.

Take watching sports, for example. What starts out as a great way to kick back and enjoy the company of friends can often become the centerpiece of every conversation. Sports schedules are consulted before making any other plans, and you soon find yourself obsessively connected to the television, watching teams you don't even care about. Before you know it, you discover that your child knows exactly why he loves football but has trouble communicating much about why he loves God.

Idolatry often has innocent-enough beginnings. But it can have disastrous effects on our relationships, the way we parent, our friendships, and our church involvement. The kingdom of Israel certainly found this to be the case. Take a look at 2 Kings 17:6-18. The Northern Kingdom, persisting in their rebellion and continuing to embrace their idols, quickly found out that there are dire consequences to idolatry and that those consequences can last for generations.

Do you think much about how the objects of your attention and affection affect those around you? Strive to view your hobbies and interests in light of Scripture. Look for the spiritual significance in the mundane elements of life, and determine what kind of legacy you're in the process of leaving. And if idolatry has taken up permanent residence in the guest room of your life, it's not too late to shoo out the unwelcome house guest.

Pause and Reflect

1   What lies at the heart of all idolatry?

2   How does 2 Kings 17:6-18 describe the Northern Kingdom's habitual idolatry?

3   How does the gospel capture our affections and destroy our idols?

What's at Stake?

Do Christians make mountains out of molehills? Sure, there are plenty of issues within Christianity that matter a lot: the Trinity, salvation by grace, the truth of Scripture, the resurrection, etc. But is the rejection of idol-worship one of the biggies? After all, how much harm can a little innocent idolatry really cause?

A lot of harm. The truth of the matter is that there's no such thing as a "little innocent idolatry." Any attention we give to idols is attention we deflect from God. When we give idols our attention, we are robbing God of the glory that is rightfully His. And God doesn't take lightly being stuck in the backseat.

That's why God prohibits idolatry in the Ten Commandments. Idolatry matters because you and I will become like what we worship. If we worship cash or convenience or comfort, then we will begin to develop appetites for them. And when we develop appetites for idols, they begin to transform us from the inside out. They invade our thoughts, attitudes, words, and actions. They take control of our relationships, time, priorities, and ambitions. Sooner or later, our idols not only own us, they become us.

Humans are slaves to appetites. That's just how we are wired. And that's why God wants us to feast on spiritual food, not idols. God wants us to set our minds on things above so we develop a hunger for the Living Bread, a thirst for the Living Water.

All throughout Scripture we see evidence of God's desire to take first place in our lives. The Messiah is the only One worth embracing in order to abandon the idols of the world. And as we loosen our death grip on the things of this world, God will help us tighten our grip on the One who's gripping us.

Pause and Reflect

1 Why does God take idolatry so seriously?

- -

2 What's at stake in our flirtation with idol-worship?

- -

3 What are idols that humans are tempted to worship today?

From Black Hole to Supernova

From the time we are born, our needs and desires take center stage above the needs and desires of anyone else. The world revolves around us—feed us, clothe us, love us, help us. You and I are born so concerned with ourselves that like a black hole, everything and everyone is pulled into the centripetal vortex of our self-centeredness.

The gospel of Jesus Christ goes the opposite direction. Instead of feeding our self-centeredness, it sends us upward and outward—upward to love God and outward to love others. Instead of feeding our centripetal desires, it puts us on a centrifugal trajectory that elevates others higher than ourselves. Paul wrote, "Do nothing out of rivalry or conceit, but in humility consider others as more important than yourselves" (Phil. 2:3).

How counterintuitive to the human nature! That others should come first. That others should be the focus of our attention. Jesus understood our basic need for survival, but He told His disciples a revolutionary truth: "Love your neighbor as yourself" (Mark 12:31). Why? Because it was in His own nature to do so.

God is always going out. Always sending, always serving. In fact, He would not tell us to do anything that He Himself did not do. Somewhere around 4 B.C., Jesus demonstrated this: He became a helpless infant in Bethlehem. Born without original sin, Christ lacked that self-centeredness that causes others to elevate idols. And 33 years later, Jesus Christ would be elevated on a cross so you and I can be showered in God's grace that transforms us into people who love God and love one another. When it comes to grace toward others, be a supernova, not a black hole.

Pause and Reflect

1   What are some spiritual disciplines that can help us elevate God and others above ourselves?

- -

2   Why do these disciplines become difficult for us?

Discussion Questions

1   Hesitating between two opinions is often a convenient way of delaying our submission to God. In what ways might our hesitation to give God our worship alert us to hidden idolatries in our life?

2   Why does God take idolatry so seriously? What is at stake in our flirtation with idol-worship? Read 1 Corinthians 10:14. What verb does Paul use in this verse? What does this suggest about how we are to deal with idolatry?

3   If Elijah believed that fire would fall from heaven and consume the sacrifice, why would he step toward it (18:36)? If he really believed that God would consume the altar, shouldn't he have stepped away from it? What kind of clue does this give us regarding Elijah's view of God's majestic yet gracious character?

4   In what ways does the God-glorifying purpose of Elijah's prayer life influence the way we pray for God to work? Are you willing to entrust your reputation to God if it will bring Him greater glory?

5   What are some ways we can keep our hearts from drifting toward other gods? How does the good news that God accepts us because of Christ's work give us a passionate affection for God more powerful than any idol?

6   Think about God's work in your own life. What are some lessons you've learned from spiritual valleys or mountaintops that you haven't considered lately? In what ways does God's work in the past influence your walk with Him today?

7   What effects does one generation have on the next? What traits are we passing down to future generations of believers?

8   The Israelites secretly sinned against the Lord (2 Kings 17:9). What secret sins or habits in your own life take precedence over your love for God?

9   How does our distinctiveness aid us in our mission as God's people?

10   How does the knowledge that we become like what we worship encourage us to more faithful worship of Jesus, the One to whose likeness we want to be conformed?

Chapter 11

Judah

The Decline and Fall of the Southern Kingdom

Voices from *the Church*

"God does not discipline us to subdue us, but to condition us for a life of usefulness and blessedness." [1]
–Billy Graham

Voices from *Church History*

"The way to Heaven is ascending; we must be content to travel up hill, though it be hard and tiresome, and contrary to the natural bias of our flesh." [2]
–Jonathan Edwards (1703-1758)

It is a dangerous thing to rebel against a holy God. Previously we saw that the Northern Kingdom (Israel) discovered this truth the hard way. Always jealous of their neighboring nations, the Israelites wanted to look and act like everyone else, adopting pagan customs and worshiping foreign idols. So God scattered the 10 tribes that made up the Northern Kingdom in 722 B.C.

What about the Southern Kingdom (Judah)? Surely they would faithfully keep the covenant, right? After all, God had made a promise to Abraham that the world's salvation would come through his descendants. But what happens when God's people are part of the problem? How can God be true to His Word to punish wrongdoing and simultaneously bring salvation through His chosen people? And what does it mean for God's purposes when His people must be disciplined? How will His rescue plan go forward? These are just a few of the questions and inner tensions that come up as we study this part of the Bible.

Here we are going to look at the fall of the Southern Kingdom in 586 B.C. and the consequences of rebelling against God's laws. Though God raised up prophets, such as Isaiah, who warned Judah of the dire consequences of idolatry, God's people continued to rebel. Yet God's judgment provided the backdrop for salvation as God promised to make a new covenant with His people that would result in the formation of new hearts.

God warned His people of the consequences of idolatry (Isa. 6:8-13).

8 *Then I heard the voice of the Lord saying: "Who should I send? Who will go for Us?"*

I said: "Here I am. Send me."

9 *And He replied: "Go! Say to these people: Keep listening, but do not understand; keep looking, but do not perceive.* 10 *Dull the minds of these people; deafen their ears and blind their eyes; otherwise they might see with their eyes and hear with their ears, understand with their minds, turn back, and be healed."*

11 *Then I said, "Until when, Lord?" And He replied: "Until cities lie in ruins without inhabitants, houses are without people, the land is ruined and desolate,* 12 *and the LORD drives the people far away, leaving great emptiness in the land.* 13 *Though a tenth will remain in the land, it will be burned again. Like the terebinth or the oak that leaves a stump when felled, the holy seed is the stump."*

God sent a prophet to His people—a man named Isaiah, the son of Amoz, who was also a prophet. We don't know much about Isaiah's life, but we do know that God gave him a very important mission. God instructed Isaiah to confront the inhabitants of Judah and Jerusalem with a sobering truth: judgment was on its way.

Isaiah's audience contained a variety of individuals, including wealthy kings and national leaders (see 2:6-22; 3:16–4:1). His audience had enjoyed a time of great prosperity. But all of this would soon change. "Oh sinful nation," warned Isaiah, "people weighed down with iniquity, brood of evildoers, depraved children! They have abandoned the LORD; they have despised the Holy One of Israel; they have turned their backs on Him" (1:4). Even dumb animals, according to Isaiah, knew better than to turn their backs on their Creator (see v. 3).

Notice the strangeness of God's call to the prophet Isaiah. After Isaiah answered the call and said, "Here I am! Send me!" God told him that the message for the Southern Kingdom would be one of judgment. In other words, Isaiah wouldn't be a prophet whose message would lead the people to repentance. Instead, his message would distance them even more from God. Judgment was coming, and Isaiah was the prophet called to announce it.

In that moment, Isaiah had to make a decision: be a prophet who would deliver a popular message for the people or be faithful to God through obedience. Would he deliver the message no matter how unpopular it would be?

The United States of America is a land of freedom. From our conception, we have been a nation of doers. We rebelled against the British monarchy, formed our own constitution, and elected our own president. We are a "pull-yourself-up-by-the-bootstraps" country.

Since we are a nation of success that thrives on increase, one of the most difficult lessons Christians in America can learn is that faithfulness is more important than success. Being obedient to God's call on our lives is more valuable than being concerned about building a life that's centered on comfort and ease.

Faithfulness to God often turns success-oriented lifestyles upside down. Instead of increase, God values decrease (see John 3:30). Instead of pursuing wealth, popularity, fame, and security, God calls us to abandon ourselves to His mission by following the movement of His Spirit, who often leads away from comfort, security, wealth, and safety. Following Jesus is a call to danger. It is a call to mission and self-denial (see Matt. 16:24). Like the nation of Judah, God calls us to abandon the pleasures of idolatry, to break our addictions to jealousy, materialism, greed, entertainment, and fornication.

This is not always the popular path. But that's the thing about Jesus. Instead of providing safety for His disciples, He warns them of martyrdom. Instead of revolting against the Roman army, He dies the death of a criminal. God is in the upside-down business—He turns human values on their head: "Whoever tries to make his life secure will lose it, and whoever loses his life will preserve it" (Luke 17:33).

Isaiah's decision between worldly success and prophetic faithfulness mirrored that of his people. Unfortunately, unlike Isaiah, the Israelites didn't make the correct choice. They said to themselves, "If we are going to be successful in Canaan, we need to look like the surrounding nations. Instead of a theocracy, we need a king. Instead of conquering our enemies, we need to adopt their worship practices." It was a terrible choice that would eventually cost them their very lives.

This passage vividly demonstrates the consequences of idolatry. Notice how Isaiah's commission and message indict idolatry. What are idols but man-made objects that have eyes but can't see, ears but can't hear, and mouths but cannot speak? This passage is about human beings becoming like what we worship. When our hearts go after idols, our hearts begin to resemble those idols. When we worship God, however, we reflect His glory.

God promised His people a new covenant that would result in new hearts (Jer. 31:31-34).

31 *"Look, the days are coming"—this is the LORD's declaration—"when I will make a new covenant with the house of Israel and with the house of Judah.* 32 *This one will not be like the covenant I made with their ancestors when I took them by the hand to bring them out of the land of Egypt—a covenant they broke even though I had married them"—the LORD's declaration.* 33 *"Instead, this is the covenant I will make with the house of Israel after those days"—the LORD's declaration. "I will put My teaching within them and write it on their hearts. I will be their God, and they will be My people.* 34 *No longer will one teach his neighbor or his brother, saying, 'Know the LORD,' for they will all know Me, from the least to the greatest of them"—this is the LORD's declaration. "For I will forgive their wrongdoing and never again remember their sin."*

Covenants exist in many forms. For those who want to be married, you need more than just a preacher and a set of vows. The law requires both parties to sign a formal contract binding the two individuals together. Unfortunately, that's a covenant too many people fail to take seriously.

Psalm 25:14 states: "The secret counsel of the LORD is for those who fear Him, and He reveals His covenant to them." God lived up to this statement. He formed a covenant with Abraham: "I am God Almighty. Live in My presence and be blameless. I will establish My covenant between Me and you, and I will multiply you greatly" (Gen. 17:1-2). He made a covenant with Moses: "Look, I am making a covenant. I will perform wonders in the presence of all your people that have never been done in all the earth or in any nation. All the people you live among will see the LORD's work, for what I am doing with you is awe-inspiring" (Ex. 34:10). And God also entered into a covenant with David (2 Sam. 7:8-16).

God never broke His end of the covenant. Yahweh remained faithful to His word even when His people abandoned Him and worshiped other gods. In His holiness, God must punish sin. And yet God must also keep His promise to Abraham to bring about salvation through His chosen people. So how can God be faithful to His promises *and* punish the sin of His people?

The answer comes by way of a promise given to the prophet Jeremiah. Even though judgment was on its way and God's people were about to go into captivity, God promised His people a new covenant. He promised to bring about reconciliation and restoration. He would not discipline them forever. Instead, He would replace their sinful, stubborn hearts with new hearts that know God and are known by Him.

Previously we talked about how humans are prone to spiritual amnesia— forgetting to obey the commands of God. Here we discover that in spite of Israel's rebellion, in spite of their rejection of God's laws, Yahweh would "never again remember their sin." What a thought! That God—the omniscient Mind who created the universe—is capable of forgetting. And what does God choose to forget? "For I will be merciful to their wrongdoing, and I will never again remember their sins" (Heb. 8:12). And again, "I will never again remember their sins and their lawless acts" (10:17). In both the Old and New Testaments, we discover this fascinating characteristic of God—His willingness to never hold our sins against us because of what He has done for us in Christ.

The graciousness of God in forgetting our sins should motivate us to "lay aside every weight and the sin that so easily ensnares us" (12:1). Because God has given us new natures, complete with new hearts and minds, we have the privilege of tearing down the idols in our lives. And we have the task of elevating God in our speech, in our actions, in our attitudes, and in our careers.

God called His people to repentance by exalting His own gracious character (Joel 2:12-13).

12 *Even now—this is the* LORD'*s declaration—turn to Me with all your heart, with fasting, weeping, and mourning.* 13 *Tear your hearts, not just your clothes, and return to the* LORD *your God. For He is gracious and compassionate, slow to anger, rich in faithful love, and He relents from sending disaster.*

Another prophet during this time was Joel, and the passage above from the book that bears his name stands as a good summary of God's message to His people *through all the prophets*: "Return to Me! Come back!" It's the cry of a God who loves His people.

Notice that God says, "Tear your hearts, not just your clothes." God was not interested in outward signs. He was not interested in the facades His people were constructing. Instead, He wanted their hearts to break because of their sins. He wanted them to feel the heaviness in their idolatry that He felt. God was jealous of their attention, and He sought inward, authentic repentance, not just outward manifestations of guilt.

God's call to His people through His prophets is based in His gracious nature. As He calls, He reminds His people of their identity by focusing on His identity. He is the God who revealed Himself to Moses—the God who is gracious and slow to anger. Even as He threatens to unleash His just judgment, He pleads with His people to repent. His pleading is the expression of His gracious and compassionate heart.

God judged His people through the exile (2 Chron. 36:15-21).

15 *But Yahweh, the God of their ancestors sent word against them by the hand of His messengers, sending them time and time again, for He had compassion on His people and on His dwelling place.* 16 *But they kept ridiculing God's messengers, despising His words, and scoffing at His prophets, until the* LORD'*s wrath was so stirred up against His people that there was no remedy.* 17 *So He brought up against them the king of the Chaldeans, who killed their choice young men with the sword in the house of their sanctuary. He had no pity on young men or young women, elderly or aged; He handed them all over to him.* 18 *He took everything to Babylon—all the articles of God's temple, large and small, the treasures of the* LORD'*s temple, and the treasures of the king and his officials.* 19 *Then the Chaldeans burned God's temple. They tore down Jerusalem's wall, burned down all its palaces, and destroyed all its valuable articles.*

20 *He deported those who escaped from the sword to Babylon, and they became servants to him and his sons until the rise of the Persian kingdom.* 21 *This fulfilled the word of the LORD through Jeremiah and the land enjoyed its Sabbath rest all the days of the desolation until 70 years were fulfilled.*

From the moment in the garden of Eden when Adam and Eve ate the forbidden fruit, exile has always been a part of human DNA: "So the LORD God sent him away from the garden of Eden to work the ground from which he was taken. He drove man out and stationed the cherubim and the flaming, whirling sword east of the garden of Eden to guard the way to the tree of life" (Gen. 3:23-24). Since this initial exile, humans have been constantly in a state of motion, longing to return to the garden from which we were once ejected.

Israel's exile from Jerusalem mimicked their ancestors' exile from Eden. They had rebelled against the commandments of God, but instead of an angel holding a flaming sword, it was King Nebuchadnezzar who brought the sword against them. When the armies of Babylon entered the walls of Jerusalem, they showed no mercy to her inhabitants. No one was safe. The elderly and the young alike were slaughtered. The virgins were taken. The prophets were ridiculed. Young men were even murdered in the sacred sanctuary of Solomon. It was carnage. The walls that had protected God's people from neighboring nations were destroyed. The temple that had enjoyed God's holy presence was burned. Everything valuable in the city was hauled off to Babylon, including the Jews who had survived this monumental massacre. It was Eden all over again.

But exile was not God's final word. The Creator would not let sin stand in the way of His desire to save His people. The inhabitants of Jerusalem would taste the consequences of their sin so that they might develop a hunger for *Living Bread* (see John 6:51). God's people were disciplined so that they might once again thirst for the God who would later answer to the name *Living Water* (see John 4).

And the exiles in Babylon became very thirsty: "By the rivers of Babylon— there we sat down and wept when we remembered Zion" (Ps. 137:1). No longer could God's people worship in the temple. No longer could they "bow down toward [God's] holy temple and give thanks" (138:2). Judgment was upon them, and the generation that had wanted so much to be like the other nations found themselves living in the very heart of one.

For God's people, exile is a present reality. Christians are constantly traveling, constantly yearning to be whole and holy. We are pilgrims on a quest for home. In fact, one of the ways we can detect spiritual sluggishness is when we stop moving. It's when we stop hungering after God, when we fail to enter His presence through the reading of His Word. In those stagnant moments, we are vulnerable to the threats of the world, the flesh, and the Devil. That's why Paul urged Christians to keep traveling, to "run in such a way to win the prize" (1 Cor. 9:24), "forgetting what is behind and reaching forward to what is ahead" (Phil. 3:13).

A day is coming when human exile will finally end. A day is coming when Christ will return to this earth, and God will once again restore the intimate fellowship that He initially designed for His creation to experience. Until that day, we should avoid the mistakes of Israel. They "hung up [their] lyres on the poplar trees" (Ps. 137:2), but we should sing praises to God, even while living in a foreign land. For Christ has entered this foreign land to save us from captivity. Jesus traveled to the world for the world so that "everyone who believes in Him will not perish but have eternal life" (John 3:16).

Conclusion

The same fire God sent from heaven to prove His existence to Elijah's enemies was the same fire God sent from heaven to destroy the cities of Sodom and Gomorrah. Some generations abandoned false idols and embraced the one true God. Other generations, however, abandoned the God of Abraham, Isaac, and Jacob—the God from whom angels had to shield themselves—and they worshiped false idols and practiced pagan rituals. Yet even though Israel wavered between judgment and restoration, between discipline and repentance, the holiness of God never changed. The faithfulness of God proved constant, despite the fickleness of His people.

Every day, you and I are given the opportunity to choose the path of obedience, to progress in our spiritual pilgrimage. God does not call us to be static saints. We are constantly on the move—growing in our understanding of Him, talking to Him in our prayers, crawling and climbing over obstacles and challenges. Because the presence of God extends everywhere, even unto the very ends of the earth, we can travel through this world as pilgrims with a purpose, as men and women on a mission.

Devotions

MOUTHPIECES OF GOD

In 1846, Belgian clarinetist Adolphe Sax patented a hybrid instrument that could be played in both woodwind and brass orchestras. The result: the saxophone. Over the years, the saxophone would be incorporated into military bands, jazz bands, woodwind orchestras, and a variety of symphonic arrangements. One of the most important characteristics of a saxophone is its mouthpiece, which allows air to flow over a reed, thus creating the necessary vibrations for sound to occur.

The prophets in the Old Testament were the mouthpieces of God. In Deuteronomy 18:18, God told His people, "I will raise up for them a prophet like you from among their brothers. I will put My words in his mouth, and he will tell them everything I command him." God lived up to His promise.

During the reign of King Hezekiah, God raised up a prophet named Isaiah who prophesied that the Babylonian army would destroy Jerusalem and enslave the people of Judah. It was devastating news: judgment was on its way because God's people had rebelled against the laws He had given them. The nation of Judah had adopted the pagan rituals of the Canaanites, and now God would discipline His chosen nation and bring them back to Himself.

It's easy to imagine that this event has nothing to do with us today. But the reality is that God meant what He said, "Do not have other gods besides Me" (Ex. 20:3). The fall of the Southern Kingdom reminds us that God takes sin seriously. He wants us to live in obedience to His call on our lives, even when it's not popular, even when it costs us everything.

Pause and Reflect

1   What has Christianity cost you?

- -

2   God can speak to us through the wise, biblical counsel of trustworthy believers. Is there a particular individual whom God has used to influence your spiritual progress? If so, how?

DESTRUCTION VS. RESTORATION

What comes to your mind when you hear the word *restoration*? Some people might think about a marriage that was crumbling but then was restored. Others might think of the devastation that a natural disaster causes and the restoration that is needed to rebuild a community.

Restoration is not natural for humans. From the moment Adam and Eve sinned in the garden of Eden, humans have spent the majority of their energy destroying, not restoring. Solomon was correct: "There is certainly no righteous man on the earth who does good and never sins" (Eccl. 7:20). Paul agreed: "There is no one righteous, not even one" (Rom. 3:10). War, murder, torture, hatred, greed, lust, idolatry. Humans have proven themselves to be continually capable of all these sins and more. In fact, these evils come quite naturally for us.

But God has always been interested in restoring what humans damage. He's interested in ushering light into the dark places of our lives—the secret places—and healing the broken pieces of our lives. After all, God entered this world as a human being to do just that. On the cross, God demonstrated His desire to restore the relationship between humanity and Himself. And He didn't stop until it was finished.

Even though God raised up Isaiah and Jeremiah to warn His people of impending judgment, He also gave them a message of hope. Hope that one day the Israelites would see freedom again. Hope that in the future they would be restored not only to their homeland but also to the covenant relationship they once experienced with Yahweh. It was a hope worth hoping in.

Pause and Reflect

1   What relationships do you have that need to be restored?

- -

2   In what ways can we as Christians bear testimony to our restored relationship with God? To God's plan to restore the world?

Mission of Love

The love of God is one of the greatest themes in Scripture. It's found on virtually every page of the Bible, from Genesis to Revelation. The prophets demonstrated it; the Gospel writers recorded it. The apostle Paul even dedicated an entire chapter to the kind of love Christians can acquire because of its origin in God (see 1 Cor. 13).

Long before sin entered the world, God basked in the love that He had for Himself. Long before God's people rejected His laws and provoked the Lord to anger, the three Persons of the Trinity existed in perfect harmony—a community of love between the Father, the Son, and the Holy Spirit. While God's justice would later be highlighted by His people's sin, God's love endured from before the creation of time itself.

That's why God went to such drastic measures to restore the love that could be expressed between Creator and creation. God sent His Son, Jesus Christ, on a rescue mission of love. Unlike Nebuchadnezzar, who took people into captivity, Christ used His kingship to offer restoration, not retaliation. It was love, not justice, that Jesus extended to His people. Justice is what's deserved: "The wages of sin is death" (Rom. 6:23). But God doesn't give us what we deserve: "The gift of God is eternal life."

As God's messengers on earth, you and I are called to live lives of love, lives of patience, kindness, gentleness, and self-control. We are called to extend God's love to a world that knows only hate. Like Isaiah, our task is to spread a message of warning, a message of repentance, a message of hope in the One who promised to come again to earth to reclaim His wandering exiles.

Ask God to sensitize your heart to the needs of your community, and pray for strength to take forth the gospel message, even when it's not popular.

Pause and Reflect

1   When was the last time you shared the gospel with someone who was not a Christian?

---

2   In what ways can your life back up your presentation of the gospel?

DISCUSSION QUESTIONS

1   Throughout the Old Testament, a prophet was considered to be the mouthpiece of God. God told Isaiah, "I have put My words in your mouth" (Isa. 51:16). What is the danger of putting our words in God's mouth?

2   How does Isaiah's commission influence the way we look at our call to evangelize? How does understanding God's role in salvation free us to focus on being faithful witnesses who entrust the results to Him?

3   Why did hearing God's Word through the prophet Isaiah make the hearts of the people hard and callous? In what ways was Isaiah's prophetic ministry part of God's judgment of His people's sin?

4   In what ways have you chosen faithfulness over worldly success? Can God use successes in our lives to accomplish His will? If so, how?

5   Love "does not keep a record of wrongs" (1 Cor. 13:5). Is this characteristic of love present in your own life? In what ways does God's forgiveness for you help you forget the sins committed against you?

6   Do you really believe God is capable of forgetting anything? What does God mean when He says, "I will never again remember their sins" (Heb. 8:12)? What effect should this have on our sanctification?

7   Why is it easy to go through the motions of Christianity without truly allowing God to change us? What are the dangers of this type of lifestyle?

8   In what ways does the righteous love of God serve as the basis for our mission efforts?

9   How does God's judgment shine light on His character? How does God's mercy illuminate His character? Are these different characteristics at odds? Why or why not?

10   The Southern Kingdom's situation was dire but never hopeless. How did God bring hope through judgment? Why does God always preserve a remnant of His people?

Chapter 12

The Exile

God Prepares His People for Deliverance

VOICES FROM *Church History*

"The winter prepares the earth for the spring: so doth afflictions sanctified prepare the soul for glory."[1]
–Richard Sibbes (1577-1635)

VOICES FROM *Church History*

"Promises, though they be for a time seemingly delayed, cannot be finally frustrated…The heart of God is not turned though His face be hid; and prayers are not flung back, though they be not instantly answered."[2]
–Timothy Cruso (circa 1656-1697)

At 9:02 a.m. on April 19, 1995, a Ryder truck containing 5,000 pounds of explosives detonated beside the Alfred P. Murrah Federal Building in Oklahoma City. The blast injured 684 people and claimed the lives of 168, including 19 children. It was the most destructive act of terror in the United States, surpassed only by the attacks on September 11 some six years later.

If you go to the Oklahoma City National Memorial today, you will see a tree standing tall at ground zero. It's called the survivor tree. Even though the explosion damaged 324 buildings in the surrounding area, this American elm survived the blast because its roots branched deeply into the ground. For this reason, it stands as a monument of hope—a visible expression of survival amidst the destruction.

The Northern and Southern Kingdoms of Israel experienced catastrophic disaster when the Assyrians and the Babylonians conquered them in the 8th and 6th centuries b.c. However, God preserved a remnant—a group of survivors who went into exile. Many of these exiles would die in foreign lands, having never seen the promised redemption. These people were caught between two worlds: the world they knew back in Israel and the world where they had been taken. A few exiles would live to see God deliver His people from the hands of captivity. But most had to remain faithful to the Lord in the midst of a pagan and foreign land.

Throughout the Old Testament, God's desire to save a remnant from utter annihilation is evident. From Noah being preserved from worldwide destruction (Gen. 6) to the remnant of surviving exiles, such as Daniel and Ezekiel, God never allowed His people to be completely destroyed. Even though the ultimate consequence of sin is death, God kept a remnant for His glory and the good of the world.

Previously we discovered the consequences that came from rebelling against God's commands. We saw how the Southern Kingdom of Judah fell into the hands of the Babylonians in 586 b.c. and how the king of the Chaldeans slaughtered God's people in the temple where they worshiped.

Here we see how the surviving children of Israel remained faithful to God while living in captivity. By looking at Daniel and Ezekiel, we will see how the Jewish people trusted in God to fulfill His promises. As we study the Word together, ask God to open your heart to discover new ways to depend on His love and His leadership in times of great difficulty. As the Puritan expression goes: It is in the deepest wells that the stars shine the brightest.

Even in difficult circumstances, God's people trust in the goodness of His Word (Dan. 1:8-17).

8 *Daniel determined that he would not defile himself with the king's food or with the wine he drank. So he asked permission from the chief official not to defile himself.* 9 *God had granted Daniel favor and compassion from the chief official,* 10 *yet he said to Daniel, "My lord the king assigned your food and drink. I'm afraid of what would happen if he saw your faces looking thinner than those of the other young men your age. You would endanger my life with the king."*

11 *So Daniel said to the guard whom the chief official had assigned to Daniel, Hananiah, Mishael, and Azariah,* 12 *"Please test your servants for 10 days. Let us be given vegetables to eat and water to drink.* 13 *Then examine our appearance and the appearance of the young men who are eating the king's food, and deal with your servants based on what you see."* 14 *He agreed with them about this and tested them for 10 days.* 15 *At the end of 10 days they looked better and healthier than all the young men who were eating the king's food.* 16 *So the guard continued to remove their food and the wine they were to drink and gave them vegetables.*

17 *God gave these four young men knowledge and understanding in every kind of literature and wisdom. Daniel also understood visions and dreams of every kind.*

According to Mosaic law, Jews were forbidden to eat pork or other forms of unclean food (see Lev. 11; Deut. 14). However, when God's people were transplanted from their homeland in 586 B.C., it became difficult for them to obey these dietary restrictions.

No one felt the pressure of this dilemma more than the prophet Daniel. When the Babylonian army took the inhabitants of Judah into captivity, Daniel and his three friends were among those in exile. The exile was God's judgment on Israel because of their sin, but it was not the end for the nation. While Daniel was living in Babylon, he maintained a lifestyle of obedience to God's Word, even though it contradicted the laws of the land.

We don't know the exact reason for the uncleanness of the Babylonian meat. Perhaps the blood had not been properly drained in accordance with the laws prescribed in Leviticus 17:13-14. Or perhaps King Nebuchadnezzar prepared a feast of pork tenderloins. Either way, the Jews would not have been able to partake in the meal.

Because of this, Daniel approached the chief guard and proposed a fascinating challenge. Because Daniel and his three friends had found favor in the eyes of the guard, they were granted permission to eat only vegetables.

The story of Daniel shows that God gives us wisdom and resolve when we are tempted to conform to the surrounding culture. God vindicated Daniel's obedience by giving him and his friends a measure of health surpassing the others.

The point of Daniel's story isn't that we should muster up additional courage and seek to remain faithful through our own willpower; it's to notice how Daniel (unlike Adam and Eve in the garden) trusted that God's Word was good and His commands were righteous. Like the other heroes of the Old Testament, Daniel points us forward to Jesus.

Furthermore, we see in this passage a terrific example of God's faithfulness to Daniel in the way He gives the prophet health. In a sense, this story points forward to the redemption that every Christian will experience when God restores to humanity the perfection that our sin has destroyed. According to Isaiah, "The wolf will live with the lamb, and the leopard will lie down with the goat. The calf, the young lion, and the fatling will be together, and a child will lead them. The cow and the bear will graze, their young ones will lie down together, and the lion will eat straw like the ox" (11:6-7).

Even in difficult circumstances, God is working to fulfill His good promises (Ezek. 37:1-14).

1 *The hand of the LORD was on me, and He brought me out by His Spirit and set me down in the middle of the valley; it was full of bones. 2 He led me all around them. There were a great many of them on the surface of the valley, and they were very dry. 3 Then He said to me, "Son of man, can these bones live?"*

I replied, "Lord GOD, only You know."

4 He said to me, "Prophesy concerning these bones and say to them: Dry bones, hear the word of the LORD! 5 This is what the Lord GOD says to these bones: I will cause breath to enter you, and you will live. 6 I will put tendons on you, make flesh grow on you, and cover you with skin. I will put breath in you so that you come to life. Then you will know that I am Yahweh."

7 So I prophesied as I had been commanded. While I was prophesying, there was a noise, a rattling sound, and the bones came together, bone to bone. 8 As I looked, tendons appeared on them, flesh grew, and skin covered them, but there was no breath in them. 9 He said to me, "Prophesy to the breath, prophesy, son of man. Say to it: This is what the Lord GOD says: Breath, come from the four winds and breathe into these slain so that they may live!" 10 So I prophesied as He commanded me; the breath entered them, and they came to life and stood on their feet, a vast army.

11 *Then He said to me, "Son of man, these bones are the whole house of Israel. Look how they say, 'Our bones are dried up, and our hope has perished; we are cut off.'* 12 *Therefore, prophesy and say to them: This is what the Lord God says: I am going to open your graves and bring you up from them, My people, and lead you into the land of Israel.* 13 *You will know that I am Yahweh, My people, when I open your graves and bring you up from them.* 14 *I will put My Spirit in you, and you will live, and I will settle you in your own land. Then you will know that I am Yahweh. I have spoken, and I will do it." This is the declaration of the Lord.*

Any osteologist (a specialist in bones) worth her salt will tell you that once a human being dies, decomposition immediately begins to occur. Once the heart stops pumping blood through the body, the chemical composition of the body changes. The change in the pH level causes the cells to lose their structural integrity. The skin begins to deteriorate, and eventually the lack of oxygen within the body leads to microbial proliferation. After a few days, the body undergoes active and advanced decay followed by the gradual disintegration of the skeleton. The saying is true: "Ashes to ashes, dust to dust."

Ezekiel's vision of the valley of dry bones reverses the process of death. Instead of decomposition, God *composes*. Instead of decay, God restores. Ezekiel looked out upon a valley of dry bones. These bones represented the nation of Israel, a nation that had been slaughtered at the hands of the Babylonians. And in Ezekiel's vision, God tells him, "Prophesy concerning these bones and say to them: Dry bones, hear the word of the Lord...I will cause breath to enter you, and you will live" (vv. 4-5).

After God's word went forth from the lips of Ezekiel, a rattling sound could be heard. Bones joined together. Ribs and collarbones, kneecaps and shoulder blades—they began to re-socket themselves. And when the skeletons had been fully repaired, sinews and muscles began to grow upon them—biceps, triceps, deltoids, sternocleidomastoids, and calf muscles found their proper places. Then blood vessels branched throughout the lifeless bodies. Skin, hair, and fingernails began to form.

But after everything had come back together, something was still missing. Even though the bodies were fully reconstructed according to the correct anatomy, life was still far from their lips.

That's when God said to Ezekiel, "Prophesy to the breath, prophesy, son of man. Say to it: This is what the Lord GOD says: Breath, come from the four winds and breathe into these slain so that they may live!" (v. 9). At that moment, another noise could be heard. A gasp must have come from the lungs of a thousand warriors. It's the sound that you hear from a drowning individual who finds that precious breath of air. And then just like God had "breathed the breath of life into his nostrils, and the man became a living being" (Gen. 2:7), the valley of dry bones became a living, breathing, active army of men.

Ezekiel's vision of restoration reflected an ancient prophecy—that at the end of Israel's exile, God's people would once again see the promised salvation of the Lord. The name of the Lord would once again be glorified. It was a precious promise—the hope of every heart—that the kingdom that had fallen into captivity would one day be unified again beneath the arms of a protective Shepherd. No longer would Daniels and Ezekiels be required to live in pagan cultures, for a day would come when God's people would be allowed to return to their homeland and practice their religion with freedom.

Decomposition was not part of God's original design for creation. It was only after sin entered the world that death and decomposition became a reality. That's why the hope for restoration does not only belong to the exiles who were living in Babylon during Ezekiel's time. We as followers of Christ claim the same hope—hope that we too may experience the life-giving restoration that comes from Jesus Christ.

Death is a form of exile, but one day, death will die. Christians will be given new bodies—resurrected bodies. One day, "He will wipe away every tear from their eyes. Death will no longer exist" (Rev. 21:4). We who are exiles will be home.

But until then, God is working to fulfill His good promises in the world. Even in the midst of our captivity, as we are caught between two worlds, God ushers hope into hopeless situations. He injects light into the darkest of circumstances.

Through the power and truth of the Word of God and the presence of the Holy Spirit, you and I are becoming more alive each day. When we become Christians, God raises us from spiritual death. As our old nature is dying, our new nature is growing. Our minds are being reconstituted. Our hearts are being revived. And God is putting His words in our mouths so we can offer a message of hope and life in a world of death and decay.

Faithfulness to the covenant results in life.

In 1818, Mary Shelley published a novel about a scientist named Victor Frankenstein who, after experimenting with the decomposition of living creatures, attempted to create his own creature. Through the combination of electrical current and dismembered body parts, Frankenstein's attempt to create life resulted in the creation of a hideously ugly monster that eventually turned against its master. *Frankenstein* is a story about a good idea that went terribly awry when humanity tried to accomplish what only God could create—life.

In the Scripture passages above, we've seen that God is the One who gives life. Daniel's testimony shows us that no matter how clever or intellectual we are, only God possesses the power to truly create. Daniel and his three friends trusted God to bring life and vitality to their bodies. And God proved Himself faithful in doing so. The same life-giving power that Ezekiel witnessed in a vision, Daniel discovered in reality. And after the tenth day of eating vegetables and drinking only water, Daniel and his friends "looked better and healthier than all the young men who were eating the king's food" (Dan. 1:15).

Ezekiel's vision teaches us that when God is faithful to His end of the covenant, life emerges where there was only death. Unlike Frankenstein, who attempted to emulate God's power by creating life, true life only comes from the One who created everything. And not only does God create us by giving us life, He *re*creates us by making us into the image of Jesus Christ.

The God who created the earth and separated it from the sea is the same God who creates new natures within us that are separate from our old natures. Just like Ezekiel's vision when God put back together the dry bones, when you and I commit our lives to becoming more like Christ, God begins the process of putting back together what sin and death tore apart. He begins putting our attitudes back together. Our ambitions and our desires find their proper place. Another word for this is *sanctification*—the process of becoming like Jesus Christ.

On this side of heaven, sin will always remain with us. We will not escape it entirely. But God's faithfulness to the covenant ensures the result of life. That's why in the new heavens and new earth, we are promised brand new bodies, glorified bodies that sin cannot influence or deteriorate.

Ezekiel's vision foreshadows the coming of a Messiah who would bring life to a lifeless people—who would heal the sick, touch the leper, restore the fallen, and raise the dead. Everywhere Christ went during His ministry, life was on display. Wherever Jesus goes, life goes.

That's why Christians need not be afraid of death. In our culture, many people don't know how to handle death. It mystifies us. We shy away from speaking about it, but we spend millions of dollars purchasing books about people who claim to have died and come back. So when we consider our own death, often our response is fear, not faith.

But even in the face of death, Christians can experience the life that only God offers. Even when the cancer has spread too far and the disease has done its worst, there is light and life at the end of this journey. God has promised us a world without decomposition or decay. A world where bones will not rattle and joints will not ache. The good news of Ezekiel and the promise of Daniel is that another world is coming, a world without end.

Conclusion

God raised up the Assyrian and Babylonian armies because Israel and Judah had forgotten to obey the laws God had given them. They had rejected their first love and replaced Him with the gods of pagan nations. They had disobeyed God's command to destroy the people of Canaan (see Josh. 9:24), and instead of wiping them out, they married into their families and began practicing pagan rituals. God's people even sacrificed their own children to appease foreign gods.

Discipline was the only course of action. And yet Ezekiel and Daniel show us that even in the midst of disciplinary action, God desired to keep a remnant of people for Himself. Even when His people were slaughtered and taken into exile, God continued to live up to His end of the covenant that He made with their ancestors. Dry bones were brought back to life in Ezekiel. Living bones were made to appear healthy in Daniel. And throughout the entirety of their captivity, God's people chose the path of faithfulness to the law over the path of compromise to the culture.

Even when you and I choose to rebel against the law of God and suffer the consequences for our actions, God is still faithful. God still desires to restore us and to give us life. His faithfulness and His promise of restoration is the basis for our heartfelt desire and willingness to obey Him—no matter what He calls us to do.

Devotions

THE THING ABOUT PENDULUMS

In 1602, Galileo wrote a letter to a friend explaining the nature and physics of a pendulum. Years later, his work was applied in clocks, in medicine as a pulse meter, and in music via the metronome—a device that keeps time by swinging a weight from a pivot point.

In the Scriptures, it seems that God's people were always swinging back and forth, always oscillating between obedience to God and conformity to surrounding cultures. Israel's journey to and their subsequent conquest of the land of Canaan provide good examples of this. At first, Israel hesitated to obey God's command to enter the land (see Num. 14). There were giants there, after all. However, even when they obeyed God and entered the promised land, the people wavered between obedience and disobedience. They underwent a cycle of sin—obedience, disobedience, punishment, and restoration. The pendulum was always swinging. But God remained constant in His faithfulness.

Ezekiel and Daniel lived during a time when the remaining survivors of the Babylonian captivity obeyed God and kept His commandments. At a moment of great difficulty, when the King of Babylon ordered his subjects to bow down and worship the golden idol that he had erected, Daniel's three friends continued to be faithful to the Lord (see Dan. 3). The stakes had been raised, and God demonstrated His faithfulness to them. And God continued to hold fast to His good promises to them, even in the midst of a fiery furnace.

Pause and Reflect

1   When in your life has your faithfulness to God wavered between obedience and disobedience?

- -

2   How did God prove Himself faithful to you in the midst of discipline and restoration?

Tenderized Through Tribulation

God might have originally created humans to be vegetarians (see Gen. 1:29-30), but there are few things in this world I enjoy more than a 14-ounce, medium-rare rib eye steak. Mercy! As an amateur griller, I've learned from experience that in order to cook a tender piece of meat, you need to prepare it beforehand. The type and size of meat will determine the way it should be prepared, of course. Some types of meat need only a slap and a sprinkle of seasoning. Other types need to be brined. In fact, depending on the size of the thicker cuts, often a hammer is needed in the tenderizing process.

Throughout the Babylonian captivity, God hammered His people into submission. Their idolatry had thickened their hearts, and it was time for them to repent. Yet even in the midst of their repentance process, God prepared His people for exile. He gave them the strength to live out their convictions even when it would cost them something, even when it would cost them everything.

It's God's faithfulness to His covenant that results in new life for us. As the Spirit works within us, enlivening our hearts and making us new, we seek to be faithful to God's Word and to obey His commands. On the flip side, when we stray from obedience to God and pursue the desires of our flesh, God disciplines us until we are restored.

Sometimes suffering is the salt that seasons our souls. It is often the case that God tenderizes us through tribulation, that is, He uses difficult circumstances to draw us back to Himself and to make our hearts compassionate toward others.

Pause and Reflect

1   Do you find it easier or more difficult to trust God during hardships? Why?

- -

2   What does 2 Corinthians 1:8-10 say about God's faithfulness to us during difficult circumstances?

From Exile to Eden

Ever since humans were ejected from Eden, we have been trying our best to return. Paul says in Romans 8:22, "For we know that the whole creation has been groaning together with labor pains until now." And don't we know it! From earthquakes and tsunamis to murder, rape, violence and suicide, creation is struggling to find a way out—to find a way back.

There is no way back, but God has given us a way forward. He has given us a path that leads to life and new creation. No more exile in the world. No more slavery or obituaries. No more car accidents or heart attacks. Through the atoning accomplishments of Jesus Christ on the cross, God is re-creating His creation. And He's doing it right now.

When you and I are obedient to the command "Go into all the world and preach the gospel to the whole creation" (Mark 16:15), we join in God's mission to bring His people out of exile. Like Daniel and Ezekiel, our witness in this world testifies to God's ability to make all things new through the sacrifice of Jesus Christ.

When we share the message of eternal hope with a friend or colleague—and then back up that message with our attitudes and actions, we are testifying to the power that makes dry bones live. When we invite a neighbor to join us on Sunday morning for a worship service for King Jesus, we are acting in the Spirit of the One who rescued Daniel and his three friends not only from starvation in Daniel 1 but also from annihilation in the fiery furnace in Daniel 3.

Following Christ in evangelism is the path that leads to life—not only ours but also those who have yet to believe.

Pause and Reflect

1 How did Christ overcome death?

---

2 What does this say about the way we should also overcome death?

---

3 How does the reality of judgment add urgency to our concern for unbelievers?

DISCUSSION QUESTIONS

1   Why does God insist on being faithful to the covenant He established even when His people prove unfaithful?

2   What role does hope play in our seeking to be faithful to God's commands? In what ways can we deepen "the roots" of our hope in God's promises?

3   Think about the last decision you made solely on the basis of your religious convictions. Did it have consequences? If so, what kind?

4   How can we demonstrate the truth of the gospel in ways that are comprehensible to the world and yet radically different from its values?

5   Why is it important to notice In Ezekiel 37 that the life of the bones came from the word of God? What does this passage suggest about how you and I should view and use the Holy Scriptures (see 2 Tim. 3:16)?

6   In what ways does the promise of resurrection change our view of death? Our view of life? What is the connection between regenerated hearts and lips that proclaim the good news of Jesus?

7   The Westminster Shorter Catechism states: "Man's chief end is to glorify God, and to enjoy him forever." How is this purpose for humanity stifled by sin? How is it made possible by God's work of salvation?

8   Why is it so important for Christians to approach death with confidence and faith instead of doubt and fear? What is the relationship between daily dying to our sinful nature and ultimate death?

9   Paul says in Romans 5:12, "Therefore, just as sin entered the world through one man, and death through sin, in this way death spread to all men, because all sinned." Paul also discusses the new life that comes from faith in Jesus Christ. In what other ways was Adam similar to Jesus Christ?

10 In John 5:24, Jesus says, "Anyone who hears My word and believes Him who sent Me has eternal life and will not come under judgment but has passed from death to life." Do you know someone who has not yet "passed from death to life"? In what ways is God using you to reach that individual? What is the greatest barrier to their salvation?

Chapter 13

The Return

Further Deliverance Awaited

VOICES FROM *Church History*

"You have not failed to notice that the last word of the Old Testament is 'curse,' and it is suggestive that the opening sermon of our Lord's ministry commences with the word 'Blessed.'" [1]
–Charles Spurgeon (1834-1892)

VOICES FROM *the Church*

"It is only when we grasp God's unyielding desire to be *with* us that we begin to see the ultimate purpose of the cross. It is more than a vehicle to rescue us from death; it transports us into the arms of Life." [2]
–Skye Jethani

If you ever happen to be in London, be sure to check out Room 52 in the British Museum. There you will find an ancient cylinder that describes the decree of King Cyrus the Great in 538 B.C. Written in cuneiform, this Persian decree stated that those who had been held captive in Babylon were free to return to their native lands.

For the Jews, this was fantastic news. The season of suffering had come to a close. Time to go home. And God had promised as much: "The LORD says: 'When 70 years for Babylon are complete, I will attend to you and will confirm My promise concerning you to restore you to this place'" (Jer. 29:10). No more slavery. No more religious and ethnic persecution. No longer did God's people weep by the rivers of Babylon (Ps. 137:1). Now after 70 excruciating years in captivity, the homecoming party could begin.

But the music would be far more somber than they could have ever expected. When the Jews arrived at their desolate city, they were dismayed by the destruction caused by King Nebuchadnezzar. They saw the broken remains of Solomon's temple, where their ancestors had once been slaughtered. They walked around the crumbling walls of the city and the dilapidated gates that had once shielded them from their enemies.

Thanks to Ezra and Nehemiah, they would begin rebuilding. But soon they would discover that the new temple was vastly inferior to its predecessor. The former glory of Israel had passed, and God's people began to yearn for a future kingdom in which the presence and peace of God would forever dwell with His people.

Previously we examined how the survivors of the destruction of the Northern and Southern Kingdoms of Israel remained faithful to God while living in captivity. Now we direct our attention to Israel's longing for restoration in the midst of her return from exile. Even though God's people rejoiced in their freedom, they would continue to long for the full restoration that would come through a Messiah. In the midst of rebuilding their temporary kingdom, they yearned for a greater kingdom—an eternal kingdom—in which God would reconcile humans to Himself.

VOICES FROM *the Church*

"Though there's pain in the offering, Blessed be Your name."
–Matt Redman, "Blessed Be Your Name"

God's people rejoiced in their return from exile yet longed for full restoration (Ezra 3:10-13).

10 *When the builders had laid the foundation of the LORD's temple, the priests, dressed in their robes and holding trumpets, and the Levites descended from Asaph, holding cymbals, took their positions to praise the LORD, as King David of Israel had instructed.* 11 *They sang with praise and thanksgiving to the LORD: "For He is good; His faithful love to Israel endures forever." Then all the people gave a great shout of praise to the LORD because the foundation of the LORD's house had been laid.*

12 *But many of the older priests, Levites, and family leaders, who had seen the first temple, wept loudly when they saw the foundation of this house, but many others shouted joyfully.* 13 *The people could not distinguish the sound of the joyful shouting from that of the weeping, because the people were shouting so loudly. And the sound was heard far away.*

When the Jewish exiles returned from Babylonian captivity and began constructing the new temple, they were filled with two conflicting emotions. The younger Jews rejoiced. After 70 years in Babylon, many of them had never seen Solomon's temple. They had never seen the splendor and grandeur that had been recounted to them since the days of their childhood. And after the treacherous thousand-mile pilgrimage to Jerusalem, the anticipation to build another temple had greatly escalated. When the initial construction process had ended and the younger Jews laid their eyes upon the new foundation, their hearts were overjoyed and they rejoiced.

But not all the Jews were thrilled. The elders in the crowd were old enough to remember the glory days before King Nebuchadnezzar stormed into Jerusalem with his armies. They could remember Solomon's spare-no-expense policy in decorating the first temple—the dressed masonry with carved wooden beams, the quarried stones, the olivewood cherubs, the inner golden sanctuary. It was a sacred spot—a holy hill on which the white-hot presence of Yahweh dwelled with His people.

But now as they gazed upon the new foundation, a sobering sentiment swept through the audience: sadness. The elders recognized that Jerusalem's new temple would be nothing compared to its majestic predecessor. And even though God's people had been redeemed from captivity in Babylon, their hearts continued to long for the day when true freedom would finally arrive. And so they wept.

In the upcoming years, the temple would be rebuilt. So would the walls around Jerusalem (see the Book of Nehemiah). By the time of Jesus, King Herod would undertake a massive construction project on the temple that spanned the entirety of Jesus' earthly life. No wonder the Jews were puzzled when Jesus said, "Destroy this sanctuary, and I will raise it up in three days" (John 2:19). How could such a monument be raised from the ashes in three meager days?

But Jesus was speaking about a different sanctuary—a more impressive one. *He* would be the sanctuary to rise from the grave in three days. *Christ* would be the temple that surpassed what Solomon and Herod had both erected. God's plan was to give His people a place for His presence to dwell. His plan was to give them Himself. His promise wasn't a building but a Savior.

More Scriptures About God's Temple
• Matthew 21:12-14; 24:1-2
• 1 Corinthians 3:16-17; 6:19-20
• 2 Corinthians 6:16
• Hebrews 9:24
• Revelation 21:22

God's people lived in light of the promise of God's presence and peace (Zech. 8:1-8).

1 *The word of the* LORD *of Hosts came:* 2 *"The* LORD *of Hosts says this: I am extremely jealous for Zion; I am jealous for her with great wrath."* 3 *The* LORD *says this: "I will return to Zion and live in Jerusalem. Then Jerusalem will be called the Faithful City, the mountain of the* LORD *of Hosts, and the Holy Mountain."* 4 *The* LORD *of Hosts says this: "Old men and women will again sit along the streets of Jerusalem, each with a staff in hand because of advanced age.* 5 *The streets of the city will be filled with boys and girls playing in them."* 6 *The* LORD *of Hosts says this: "Though it may seem incredible to the remnant of this people in those days, should it also seem incredible to Me?"—this is the declaration of the* LORD *of Hosts.* 7 *The* LORD *of Hosts says this: "I will save My people from the land of the east and the land of the west.* 8 *I will bring them back to live in Jerusalem. They will be My people, and I will be their faithful and righteous God."*

In 2011, the residents of Utah experienced one of the worst power outages in their history. When a windstorm swept through the Rocky Mountains in early December, 55,000 residents lost electricity. Many were exiled to cold conditions for days. "We've been roughing it for a while now," said one weary resident. "Everyone's cold." The anticipation for the return of electricity escalated until the power eventually returned to their homes in the Rocky Mountains. And when the power did return, their exile ended and life in Utah could once again resume. [3]

Having been exiled in a foreign land for 70 years, the Jews breathed a sigh of relief to hear the news that Zechariah was spreading: power would return to Mount Zion. No news could have been better than this. No rumor could have produced greater hope, for the presence and peace of God would bring light and restoration to a dark and desolate mountain.

If the mountains surrounding Israel had witnessed anything in their enduring history, they had seen firsthand the jealous zeal of Yahweh. The summit of Mount Ararat had witnessed the smile of God in the form of a rainbow as Noah and his family safely stepped onto dry land. The summit of Mount Horeb (Sinai) had seen Moses climb its peak to receive this commandment from God: "You must not bow down to them or worship them; for I, the LORD your God, am a jealous God" (Ex. 20:5). Mount Carmel also got in on the action when, at its base, God sent fire down from heaven to show the 450 prophets of Baal who was boss (1 Kings 18:20-40). God's jealousy for His people often took the form of wrath, but that jealousy also worked for the good of those He loved.

Perhaps the most favored mountain in all of Israel—Mount Moriah—had seen God's jealous love most clearly. It was on this mountain that God had instructed Abraham, "Take your son...your only son Isaac, whom you love... and offer him there as a burnt offering" (Gen. 22:2). But instead of having Abraham offer Isaac, God provided a ram. It was on this very rock that God had once appeared to David and where Solomon began construction on the temple (2 Chron. 3:1). Mount Moriah, or Mount Zion as it would later be called, became a sacred spot upon which the city of Jerusalem rested. And as the Jews left Babylon to return to this beloved mountain, the jealous love of God led the way. Power had returned to the mountain, and the dawning of a new era had arrived.

The promised future that God pledged to the Jews is the same promise that you and I can experience today. When we put our trust in Christ the King, we stand on a faith that values the eternal presence of God more than the geographic location He inhabits. Heaven itself is not our ultimate goal—God is. That's why John's descriptions of the new Jerusalem in Revelation 21 emphasized the primacy and centrality of Jesus Christ, who is in Himself the final temple.

Hundreds of years after Zechariah prophesied, Jesus would tell the Samaritan woman, "Believe Me, woman, an hour is coming when you will worship the Father neither on this mountain nor in Jerusalem" (John 4:21). No longer is Mount Zion the goal—Christ is the Rock of Ages. He is to be the object of our affection. Like Abraham, we travel "looking forward to the city that has foundations, whose architect and builder is God" (Heb. 11:10), but it's not the city we are most interested in. It's the Architect of the city, who floods the streets with His glorious presence. Power is coming to the new Jerusalem, and when we arrive, Christ will be the One who holds the ultimate interest of our hearts.

God's people looked to the kingdom that would reconcile us to God and others (Mal. 4:4-6).

4 *"Remember the instruction of Moses My servant, the statutes and ordinances I commanded him at Horeb for all Israel.* 5 *Look, I am going to send you Elijah the prophet before the great and awesome Day of the LORD comes.* 6 *And he will turn the hearts of fathers to their children and the hearts of children to their fathers. Otherwise, I will come and strike the land with a curse."*

Often called "America's pastime," baseball was one of the earliest social institutions in the United States. Established before the Civil War, baseball resembled its English counterpart, cricket, and quickly became a symbol of the American spirit.

Yet for pitchers, it's not all "peanuts and Cracker Jack." One injury, perhaps the most feared of all—the "Tommy John"—requires significant elbow reconstruction. Because a pitcher reaches back in order to propel his arm forward, the back-forth motion places tremendous stress on the elbow and shoulder. Eventually, the ulnar collateral ligament can tear, resulting in a devastating injury that has ended many athletic careers.

Malachi struggled beneath a heavy weight on his shoulders. The KJV renders the book's opening this way: "The *burden* of the word of the LORD to Israel by Malachi." What was this burden that God commanded Malachi to thrust in the direction of Israel? Malachi instructed the Jews to reach back into their history and remember God's servant Moses in order to move forward in anticipation of another prophet—John the Baptist: "Remember the instruction of Moses My servant," said God, "the statutes and ordinances I commanded him at Horeb for all Israel" (Mal. 4:4).

For Israel, memory served as an antidote to disobedience. If the Jews had only remembered the instructions God had given their forefather Moses and how, through divine providence, the Lord had delivered them from slavery, they might have avoided kindling God's wrath by offering Him leftover and blemished sacrifices (see Mal. 1:8). If the Jews had only remembered the brutality of the Babylonian captivity and how, after 70 years, God delivered His people so they could rebuild their city on a hill, they might have avoided lighting useless fires on God's altar (see 1:10).

In most Bibles, a blank page separates the Old Testament from the New Testament. That blank page represents 400 years of silence—400 years when God did not speak to His people at all. Four hundred years is a long time to endure the deafening silence of God.

But Malachi prophesied about a day when the silence would be broken. He spoke about the "Day of the LORD" in which sin and death would have no dominion: "Look, I am going to send you Elijah the prophet before the great and awesome Day of the LORD comes" (4:5). Instead of Elijah himself, God would raise up an "Elijah-like" prophet named John the Baptist, who would proclaim with great boldness the Messiah was on His way.

The coming Messiah would inaugurate God's kingdom. Instead of abolishing the law God had given His people, Christ would fulfill the law by interpreting it and then getting at the spirit behind the commandments that were given. The Messiah would bring reconciliation that would stretch vertically (God and people) as well as horizontally (reconciling people to people).

But reconciliation would carry an enormous price tag. Like Malachi, the Messiah would also carry an enormous burden on His shoulders. The Messiah would carry this burden all the way to the cross, where He would reach out His arms and suffer under the weight of the world's sin and despair.

The story doesn't end at the cross, however; there is an empty tomb. The Messiah is our Champion, and that is why you and I can place our hope in the One who promises to deliver us from the captivity of sin just as He once delivered the Jews from Babylon. The bottom line is this: The days of our earthly exile are numbered, and the "Day of the LORD" is on its way. And on that day, all things will be made new, all things will be made whole, and we will live in perfect harmony with the Holy One. Until then, we trust in the beauty of our promise-making and promise-keeping God.

Conclusion

Every year in October, Jews observe a celebration called the *Sukkot* feast—a seven-day celebration renewed at the end of Jewish captivity in Babylon and the return pilgrimage to Jerusalem. The seventh day of this feast represents the final cry of anguish of those in exile longing for salvation. For this reason, it's called *Hoshana Rabba* ("Great Salvation").

Five hundred years after the return from exile, a Prophet rode into Jerusalem. People lined the streets to see this greatly anticipated Hero, this Leader who would rescue the Jews from Roman captivity. But there was a problem. This Prophet wasn't riding on a war horse. There was no armor on His body, no weapon in His hand. Instead, the Prophet entered Jerusalem riding on a donkey—a sign of poverty and humility.

The kind of kingdom this Prophet inaugurated wasn't a dynasty of war and death. It didn't need armies or catapults. A Messiah of peace? How? But that's exactly what Jesus was, and that's precisely what Jesus brought.

In the spirit of the *Sukkot* pilgrimage, when the Jews expressed their greatest longing for salvation, robes and branches were spread across the ground as Jesus rode through the streets of Jerusalem. People shouted, "Hosanna"—the Greek word for *hoshana* and a plea for salvation. "Hosanna to the Son of David! He who comes in the name of the Lord is the blessed One!" (Matt. 21:9). For the Jews, the days of captivity and exile were over, for a Savior of the world had come to march His people to the promised land.

Devotions

UNFINISHED MASTERPIECE

Non Finito. That's Latin for "not finished," and that's exactly what happened to J. R. R. Tolkien's work *Unfinished Tales of Númenor and Middle-Earth.* Author of the famous *The Lord of the Rings* series, Tolkien died in 1973, leaving his son Christopher to publish the remainder of his works. For those of you who dream of hobbits, elves, and orcs, you might be interested to pick up this unfinished masterpiece that tells the origins of the great wizard Gandalf.

Even those who know precious little about Middle-earth can identify with Tolkien's incomplete masterpiece. At one time or another, all of us have experienced the frustration and anticipation of an unfinished project. It may have been an essay in college that wasn't yet up to par. Perhaps you pitched a presentation at work that could have benefited from a few more hours in the office. Humans have always wrestled with *non finito,* for we ourselves are unfinished creatures.

The Jews who returned from Babylon felt the burden of incompletion full force. Tasked with constructing a second temple, they soon realized that it would not live up to the grandeur of Solomon's original temple. Some wept; others rejoiced (see Ezra 3:12). But eventually, all would long for a day when a Messiah would usher in a new kingdom, complete with a new and perfect temple.

As Christians, we find ourselves continually sandwiched between Middle-earth and "new earth" (Rev. 21:1). However, God does not call us merely to wait for the new kingdom to arrive. Each of us is commanded to witness to God's restorative empire by representing the hands and feet of Christ for a world that needs healing.

Pause and Reflect

1   In what ways have you witnessed to the kingdom of God this week?

----

2   Read Romans 8:22. Why is all of creation groaning? What metaphor does Paul use to illustrate this anticipation?

LONGING, LIVING, LOOKING

In the 1994 blockbuster sensation *The Shawshank Redemption*, Tim Robbins plays the character Andy Dufresne, a banker convicted of killing his wife and sentenced to lifelong imprisonment. At one point during his imprisonment, Andy looked over at his fellow inmate Red and said, "Get busy living, or get busy dying." Shortly thereafter, Andy performed a daring escape through a narrow tunnel that he had dug in his cell.

After the miraculous deliverance from imprisonment in Babylon, the Jews had to choose: get busy living or get busy dying. Their choice involved either turning to God and living in the hope of future restoration or rebelling against God and living in disobedience to His covenant instructions. In Ezra, the Jews rejoiced in their return from exile and decided to live in a state of longing for God's restoration. In Zechariah, God's people lived in light of the promise of God's presence and peace. And in Malachi, the Jews looked to the kingdom that would reconcile humanity and divinity for all eternity.

As Christians, we are also called to long, live, and look. As unfinished creatures awaiting future perfection, we long for the day when God will give us new bodies (see 1 Cor. 15:42-44) and when we will forever bask in the worship and adoration of Christ. Even though we currently live by faith, we live in anticipation of the day when we will live by sight. And just like the Jews who looked forward to the first coming of the Messiah, we look for the second coming of the One who will come "in clouds with great power and glory" (Mark 13:26).

Pause and Reflect

1   In what ways should knowledge of Christ's second return foster within us an urgent sense of evangelism?

- -

2   If Jesus Christ were to return to earth tomorrow, how would that influence the way you act today?

SPOILER ALERT

Have you ever found yourself in a conversation about a movie you haven't seen, and then suddenly, someone gives away the surprise twist at the end of a film like *The Sixth Sense*? In order to circumnavigate this problem, blog writers insert [SPOILER ALERT] in their reviews before giving away a big surprise ending.

The Bible also contains spoiler alerts. From Genesis to Revelation, Scripture points to the future reality of Jesus Christ. In the Old Testament, the prophets pointed forward. For instance, as the Book of Malachi closes, the author directs our attention to a future event that no one could have predicted: "Look, I am going to send you Elijah the prophet before the great and awesome Day of the LORD comes" (Mal. 4:5). The coming Messiah would inaugurate a kingdom of peace long prophesied throughout the Old Testament.

In the New Testament, the writers pointed backward to Christ's first coming. Paul reminded Timothy, "Keep your attention on Jesus Christ as risen from the dead and descended from David" (2 Tim. 2:8).

But the New Testament also points us forward—and outward. And this is where mission comes in. Like the comforting words of freedom falling on the ears of those imprisoned in Babylon, we too are called to proclaim the freedom that comes from anticipating the ultimate freedom—when [SPOILER ALERT] Jesus Christ "will appear a second time, not to bear sin, but to bring salvation to those who are waiting for Him" (Heb. 9:28).

Pause and Reflect

1   What's the danger in viewing the Bible as 66 separate and unconnected books? What encouragement can you derive from viewing Scripture as a unified story?

- -

2   Do you see a tension in waiting for the end to arrive while also living in the present? Why is it essential to live according to the gospel while awaiting the fulfillment of the gospel?

DISCUSSION QUESTIONS

1   Have you ever looked forward to something with great anticipation only to be let down by the reality? How might God use our disillusionment to stir up a desire for joy that only He can give?

2   Writing about the new Jerusalem in Revelation 21:22, John penned the words "I did not see a sanctuary in it." How does John finish this statement? What is the significance of living in a temple-less Jerusalem?

3   What does it mean to be a redeemed person in an unrestored world? In what ways should this mournful joy or joyful mourning be the expression of every Christian's heart?

4   How does God's promise of future restoration give us hope in our present realities? In what ways does God's promise urge us to action?

5   What are some spiritual disciplines that can foster in us a sense of anticipation for the new heavens and new earth?

6   What is the connection between the power of God and the jealousy of God? Why is God's jealousy good news for His people? How does knowledge of God's jealousy compel us to be ministers of reconciliation?

7   Why is it often difficult to live in light of the promise of God's presence and peace? How does contemporary culture and media depict those who live with hope in God's promised future?

8   What can the memory of your past teach you about what God requires of your future?

9   How does reconciliation between people point to the reality of God's kingdom? How do we demonstrate to the world both our dissatisfaction with the world as it is in the present and our belief in the world God will bring about in the future?

10 Like the cylinder that contains the decree of King Cyrus the Great, how does God's Word free us to live in peace with others while also permitting us to prepare for future restoration? If Scripture is one long story, what would you say its primary theme would be? How do you fit into that story?

Endnotes

Chapter 1

1. Keith Whitfield, "The Triune God: The God of Mission," in *Theology and Practice of Mission*, ed. Bruce Riley Ashford (Nashville: B&H Academic, 2011), 30.
2. Carl F. H. Henry, *Aspects of Christian Social Ethics* (Grand Rapids: Baker Books, 1980), quoted in *What Were We Put in the World to Do?* by Tim Keller (Redeemer Presbyterian Church, 2006), 16.

Chapter 2

1. Augustine, *City of God*, 14:13, in *Fathers of the Church: A New Translation* (Washington, DC: Catholic University of America Press, 1947-), 14:382-83, quoted in *Genesis 1–11*, ed. Andrew Louth, vol. 1 in *Ancient Christian Commentary on Scripture: Old Testament* (Downers Grove: InterVarsity Press, 2001), 77.
2. Michael E. Wittmer, *Heaven Is a Place on Earth* (Grand Rapids: Zondervan, 2004), 180.

Chapter 3

1. Jason C. Dukes, *Live Sent: You Are a Letter* (Tucson, AZ: Wheatmark, 2009), xiv.
2. C. H. Spurgeon, "The Call of Abraham," The Spurgeon Archive [online], 10 July 1859 [cited 21 May 2012]. Available from the Internet: *www.spurgeon.org*.

Chapter 4

1. Timothy Keller, *Counterfeit Gods* (New York: Dutton, 2009), xxiv.
2. Augustine, *Tractate on the Gospel of John*, 55.1, in *Fathers of the Church: A New Translation* (Washington, DC: Catholic University of America Press, 1947-), 90:3-4, quoted in *Exodus, Leviticus, Numbers, Deuteronomy*, ed. Joseph T. Lienhard, vol. III in *Ancient Christian Commentary on Scripture: Old Testament* (Downers Grove: InterVarsity Press, 2001), 63.

Chapter 5

1. Francis A. Schaeffer, quoted in *Letters of Francis A. Schaeffer*, ed. Lane T. Dennis (Wheaton: Crossway, 1985), 202.
2. David Platt, *Radical Together* (Colorado Springs: Multnomah Books, 2011), 124.
3. Arthur Bennett, ed., *The Valley of Vision* (Carlisle, PA: The Banner of Truth Trust, 1975), 73.

Chapter 6

1. Henry T. Blackaby and Richard Blackaby, *Experiencing God Day-by-Day* (Nashville: Broadman & Holman Publishers, 1998), 213.
2. Charles H. Spurgeon, *Morning and Evening* (Peabody, MA: Hendrickson, 1991), 265.

Chapter 7

1. D. A. Carson, *The God Who Is There* (Grand Rapids: Baker Books, 2010), 83.

Chapter 8

1. Athanasius, *Festal Letters*, 5.1, in *The Resurrection Letters by Athanasius*, paraphrased and introduced by Jack N. Sparks (Nashville: Thomas Nelson, 1979), 90-91, quoted in *Psalms 1–50*, eds. Craig A. Blaising and Carmen S. Hardin, vol. VII in *Ancient Christian Commentary on Scripture: Old Testament* (Downers Grove: InterVarsity Press, 2008), 7.
2. Dietrich Bonhoeffer, *Psalms: The Prayer Book of the Bible*, trans. (Minneapolis: Augsburg Fortress, 1970), 14-15.

Chapter 9

1. Ambrose, *Six Days of Creation*, 1.4.12, in *Fathers of the Church: A New Translation* (Washington DC: Catholic University of America Press, 1947-), 42:12, quoted in *Proverbs, Ecclesiastes, Song of Solomon*, ed. J. Robert Wright, vol. IX in *Ancient Christian Commentary on Scripture: Old Testament* (Downers Grove: InterVarsity Press, 2005), 7.

Chapter 10

1. Blaise Pascal, *Thoughts*, trans. W. F. Trotter, M. L. Booth, and O. W. Wight (New York: P. F. Collier & Son Company, 1910), 325.
2. A. W. Pink, ed., *Studies in the Scriptures* 7, no. 3 (March 1928): 72.

Chapter 11

1. Billy Graham, *The Secret of Happiness* (Nashville: Thomas Nelson, 2002).
2. Jonathan Edwards, "The Christian Pilgrim," in *The Works of Jonathan Edwards, A.M.*, by Henry Rogers, vol. 1 (New York: Daniel Appleton and Co., 1835), 243.

Chapter 12

1. Richard Sibbes, "Divine Meditations," in *The Complete Works of Richard Sibbes, D.D.*, ed. Alexander Balloch Grosart (Edinburgh: James Nichol, 1864), 189.
2. Timothy Cruso, quoted in *The Treasury of David*, by C. H. Spurgeon, vol. 1 (New York: I. K. Funk & Co., 1882), 287.

Chapter 13

1. C. H. Spurgeon, "The Beatitudes" [online; cited 3 May 2012]. Available from the Internet: *preceptaustin.org*.
2. Skye Jethani, *With* (Nashville: Thomas Nelson, 2011), 110.
3. Jonelle Merrill, "Power returning to thousands of Rocky Mountain Power customers in Ogden," *ABC 4 News* [online], 3 December 2011 [cited 7 June 2012]. Available from the Internet: *www.abc4.com*.

Small Group Tips

Reading through this section and utilizing the suggested principles and practices will greatly enhance the group experience. First is to accept your limitations. You cannot transform a life. Your group must be devoted to the Bible, the Holy Spirit, and the power of Christian community. In doing so your group will have all the tools necessary to draw closer to God and to each other—and to experience heart transformation.

General Tips

• Prepare for each meeting by reviewing the material, praying for each group member, and asking the Holy Spirit to work through you as you point to Jesus each week.

• Make new attendees feel welcome.

• Think of ways to connect with group members away from group time. The amount of participation you have during your group meetings is directly related to the amount of time you connect with your group members away from the group meeting. Consider sending e-mails, texts, or social networking messages encouraging members in their personal devotion times prior to the session.

Materials Needed

• Bible

• Bible study book

• Pen/pencil

Provide Resources for Guests

An inexpensive way to make first-time guests feel welcome is to provide them a copy of your Bible study book. Estimate how many first-time guests you can expect during the course of your study, and secure that number of books. What about people who have not yet visited your group? You can encourage them to visit by providing a copy of the Bible study book.

Pray for Your Group Specifically

In a group where discussion is fostered, you'll inevitably come to learn things about people's lives. As those things come up, write them down. Pray for them throughout the week. Then, the next time you meet, pull the person aside and ask them more about their situation. Not only is there incredible value in caring for people like this, it also links them emotionally to what's going on in your group.

–Michael Kelley, *9Marks Journal* (January/February 2012)

Foster Openness and Discussion

Instead of thinking about the most effective way you can teach, think instead about what question you might ask in order to help someone else in your group articulate the information. It's okay if you stand at the front and simply give out the information, but it will be a more engaging and memorable experience if people come to the same conclusion seemingly on their own. After all, the goal is for truth to be expounded.

–Michael Kelley, *9Marks Journal* (January/February 2012)

Knowing Your Major

Every diploma represents countless hours of reading, writing, and successfully passed tests. College diplomas also represent the meeting of standards in a selected field of study. That defined field of study usually signifies a path for the future of that graduate. It is what he or she thinks they will do or become. We wouldn't expect a person who majored in physics to become a history teacher. If your group were being awarded a degree, what would be the major listed on the diploma? Would it be recognized for the study done, the reaching of others, the care for those already included, or all of these things? Take some time to evaluate your group, and begin to set in motion actions that will help you accomplish your major as a group.

How to Use This Resource

Welcome to *The Gospel Project*, a gospel-centered curriculum that dives deep into the things of God, lifts up Jesus, focuses on the grand story of Scripture, and drives participants to be on mission. This short-term resource provides opportunities to study the Bible and to encounter the living Christ. *The Gospel Project* provides you with tools and resources to purposefully study God's Word and to grow in the faith and knowledge of God's Son. And what's more, you can do so in the company of others, encouraging and building up one another.

Here are some things to remember that will help you maximize the usefulness of this resource:

Gather a Group. We grow in the faith best in community with other believers, as we love, encourage, correct, and challenge one another. The life of a disciple of Christ was never meant to be lived alone, in isolation.

Pray. Pray regularly for your group members.

Prepare. This resource includes the Bible study content, three devotionals, and follow-up questions for each chapter. Work through the chapter and devotionals in preparation for each group session. Take notes and record your own questions. Also consider the follow-up questions so you are ready to participate in and add to the discussion, bringing up your own notes and questions where appropriate.

Resource Yourself. Make good use of the additional resources available on the Web at *www.gospelproject.com/additionalresources*. Download a podcast. Read a blog post. Be intentional about learning from others in the faith.

Group Time. Gather together with your group to discuss the chapter and devotional content. Work through the follow-up questions and your own questions. Discuss the material and the implications for the lives of believers and the mission to which we have been called.

Overflow. Remember…*The Gospel Project* is not just a curriculum. WE are the project. The gospel is working on us. Don't let your preparation time be simply about the content. Let the truths of God's Word soak in as you study. Let God work on your heart first, and then pray that He will change the hearts of the other people in your group.

Old Testament Timeline

circa 2166-1805 B.C.

Place: Abraham is promised a land for his descendants; sojourn in Egypt

Important People: Abraham, Isaac, Jacob, Joseph

Important Events: God's covenant with Abraham; Sodom and Gomorrah destroyed; sacrifice of Isaac; Jacob steals blessing; Jacob's name changed to Israel; Joseph sold into slavery

Books that cover this period of history: Genesis 12–50

circa 1446 B.C.

Place: God's people rescued from slavery in Egypt

Important People: Moses, Aaron, Miriam

Important Events: God's people oppressed; Moses called as deliverer; 10 plagues in Egypt; Passover; the exodus

Books that cover this period of history: Exodus 1–18

circa 1446-1406 B.C.

Place: God's people in the wilderness before entering the promised land

Important People: Moses, Aaron, Joshua, Caleb

Important Events: Sinai covenant; Ten Commandments; tabernacle built; priesthood established and offerings prescribed; golden calf; scouting promised land and refusal to enter; wandering in the wilderness

Books that cover this period of history: Exodus 19–40; Leviticus; Numbers; Deuteronomy

circa 1406-1060 B.C.

Place: God's people take possession of the land promised to Abraham

Important People: Joshua, Caleb, Rahab, Achan, Deborah, Gideon, Samson, Naomi, Ruth, Boaz

Important Events: Crossing the Jordan; conquest of Jericho; distribution of land; death of Joshua; the judges lead Israel

Books that cover this period of history: Joshua; Judges; Ruth

circa 1105-931 B.C.

Place: God's people as a united kingdom

Important People: Hannah, Eli, Samuel, Saul, Jonathan, David, Abigail, Bathsheba, Absalom, Solomon

Important Events: Samuel's prophetic ministry; Saul anointed as first king; David kills Goliath; God's covenant with David; David's adultery with Bathsheba; Absalom's rebellion; Solomon's temple

Books that cover this period of history: 1–2 Samuel; 1 Kings; 1–2 Chronicles; Psalms; Proverbs; Ecclesiastes; Song of Songs

circa 931-722 B.C.

Place: God's people divided in North (Israel) and South (Judah)

Important People: Rehoboam, Jeroboam, Ahab and his wife Jezebel, Elijah, Elisha, Jehoshaphat

Important Events: Division of the kingdom; Elijah versus the prophets of Baal; Naboth's vineyard; Jehoshaphat's reforms; Elisha's ministry; Naaman the leper; fall of the Northern Kingdom

Books that cover this period of history: 1–2 Kings; 1–2 Chronicles

722-586 B.C.

Place: The Southern Kingdom (Judah)

Important People: Isaiah, Hezekiah, Sennacherib (Assyrian king), Josiah, Jeremiah

Important Events: Fall of Northern Kingdom to Assyria; messianic prophecies; Josiah's reforms; deportations to Babylon; new covenant promise; fall of Jerusalem

Books that cover this period of history: 2 Kings; 2 Chronicles; Amos; Jonah; Hosea; Micah; Isaiah; Nahum; Jeremiah; Zephaniah; Joel; Habakkuk

586-538 B.C.

Place: God's people exiled in Babylon

Important People: Jeremiah, Nebuchadnezzar (Babylonian king), Daniel, Ezekiel

Important Events: Daniel's ministry in Babylonian court; Ezekiel's ministry to the exiles

Books that cover this period of history: Jeremiah; Lamentations; Daniel; Obadiah; Ezekiel

538-400 B.C.

Place: God's people return to the land

Important People: Cyrus (Persian king), Ezra, Nehemiah, Esther

Important Events: Return to Jerusalem; rebuilding the temple; rebuilding walls and city; reestablishing worship

Books that cover this period of history: Haggai; Zechariah; Ezra; Nehemiah; Esther; Malachi

Group Contact Information

Name _____ Number _____
E-mail _____

Name _____ Number _____
E-mail _____

Name _____ Number _____
E-mail _____

Name _____ Number _____
E-mail _____

Name _____ Number _____
E-mail _____

Name _____ Number _____
E-mail _____

Name _____ Number _____
E-mail _____

Name _____ Number _____
E-mail _____

Name _____ Number _____
E-mail _____

Name _____ Number _____
E-mail _____

Name _____ Number _____
E-mail _____